JOCKS

ALSO BY BURT GOLDEN

Madness of March (an Amazon Best Seller)

Jericho's Walls

The Dead Listing

Dead Is Not Enough

Shadows

These titles are easily available by googling
"Burt Golden Amazon"

JOCKS

a memoir

Burt Golden

LITTLE JOHN PRESS

JOCKS is a work of nonfiction. The events are portrayed
to the best of my memory. I regret any unintentional harm
resulting from the publishing and marketing of JOCKS.

Copyright © 2021 by Burt Golden

Little John Press
Newport Beach, CA 92660

All rights reserved

Printed in the United States of America

Book design by Sasha Wizansky

ISBN 978-0-9860044-8-3

To my sons, Dane and Jay Golden,
who coaxed me to turn great dinnertime stories
into this memoir, then supported and encouraged me
during the 20 years it took to write JOCKS.

And to every jock who never gave up going after their dream.

ACKNOWLEDGMENTS

I would like to thank the following people for their help and support:

Joanne Shelley, Maddie Margarita, author Lance Charnes, Maxine Golden, and Janet Ennis.

Success is not final, failure is not fatal:

It is the courage to continue that counts.

– Winston Churchill

Prologue

I walked down the rickety stairs, following our players, one-by-one, as they ducked under the doorway after our shoot-around before the evening's game. Nerves were high. Our university had never played in the NCAA Tournament, or on national TV.

Suddenly surprised, I looked around and realized where I was.

Of course. The locker room locked away in my memory. The exact piece of cold hard floor I had left behind 20 years before. Ghosts of the past suited up in front of tall, gray metal lockers. The familiar sour smell of sweat. That Burt was a different person with dreams and a different life. So much changed, and so little.

Same marred wood table in the corner where I swung my broom. The place where Charlie handed me his tickets. Where Henry let me in, leading me to a life I could never have imagined, while living one life and creating another. I was stuck back then. Baseball was my only dream. Now, no one would believe I was back.

I reminded our players to stay off their feet when they got back to the hotel and to meet at 2:30 for our pregame meal. Then, I turned to our manager, a nice young man who dressed like an unmade bed. "I'm going for a walk upstairs. Let me know when everyone is showered up and ready to board the bus."

I made my way up aged wood stairs, then heard my footsteps echo down a wide hardwood floor in the hallway that circled the arena. Seconds later I passed an arena entrance where TV cameras were being rolled into the massive structure, and the overhead scoreboard blinked.

Dreams of green uniforms, Henry knocking out a teammate, the squeak of Converse All-Star shoes, Coach Belko yelling, and me trying to find my way.

I continued around a curve and came upon two long rows of large black and white photos encased in glass, brightened by overhead lights. A sign on top read "Oregon Athletic Hall of Fame." I scanned the photos. One photo stopped me in my tracks.

Otis Davis, Track, 1958-1959. Otis was kneeling on a clay track in front of Oregon's Hayward Stadium with a broad smile. As I gazed at my reflection in the glass, memories lit the corners of my mind. Henry, Charlie, Padovan, Bowerman, Otis. All complete originals in a unique time—and a moment where the course of my life changed.

Now they would be called student/athletes. Back then they called us jocks.

Chapter 1

JANUARY 5, 1958

BOYLE HEIGHTS, CALIFORNIA

It was a bright and sunny January morning when I waved goodbye to my mother, dad, and younger brother Mike, standing on the porch of our duplex. I was leaving my America—Boyle Heights, a community in East Los Angeles. I was on my way to pick up Henry Ronquillo and make a long drive through the middle of California and beyond, to the University of Oregon in Eugene, a step toward my lifetime dream of playing pro ball. Oregon played winning baseball, had my major, and offered me a scholarship. Henry and I had no maps, but I sensed that if I drove north long enough on Highway 99, we would get there.

Henry and I were once co-conspirators in junior college when we "borrowed" the stadium jeep and drove up the hills behind the college to chase the cows. Now he played basketball for the university, and had been home recovering from a badly sprained ankle.

In November, when I called to tell him that I was considering accepting a baseball scholarship at Oregon, he said, "Oregon is another world, man. There's no place like Boyle Heights." I understood the latter. I was coming from a community of Chicanos, Jews, Japanese, Armenians, Italians, Russians, and African-Americans. The people I knew were raw, abrupt, honest, diverse, stressed, friendly, volcanic, street-smart, tough, limited, religious, proud, and cornered—a meld of working class and working poor who survived the depression, World War II and the internment camps. I was a little bit of everything, with a tinge of Chicano machismo and Jewish chutzpah thrown in.

I was lucky to get out of East L.A. College at all because I refused to turn down the student union jukebox after I turned it all the way up. Problem was, I had refused Dean Fields, the Dean of Students. Two days later, I received a letter from her notifying me that I was on disciplinary probation, which meant no university baseball coach would offer a scholarship to a troublemaker. With my back against the wall, I buried my head in the college rulebook and I learned that if Dean Fields signed off on my application to run for student body president, I would be off disciplinary probation. A few days later, with my heart in my mouth, I handed her my application to run for that office. And Dean Fields surprised me by approving it, ending my probation status. The hell of it was that I was almost elected to the office, even though I was leaving the school.

* * *

Now I was pulling up my roots, leaving family, friends, and a special relationship for something no bookie would give odds on. It was like moving to Sweden or something. Far out. I didn't care if only five to ten percent of students who had attended a junior college would ever get a bachelor's degree, or that there were miniscule odds of playing in "The Show." I was going.

* * *

By the time we crossed into Oregon late that night, I had already seen enough small towns, grain elevators, tumbleweeds, abandoned junkyard cars, and snow-packed pine trees to fill a lifetime.

Long after Highway 99 suddenly became Highway 5 and we had begun our descent from a pass, Henry told me about his family moving to California. They were laborers, he said, picking almonds in the central valley and living in a migrant shack. Upon hearing that story,

I thought we had something in common—border crossings. So I said, "My grandmother crossed a border, also. Russian. 1907. She and her two-year-old daughter, my future mother, were hiding in a hay wagon and were stopped at the border by a soldier who stabbed the haystack with a pitchfork to make sure no one was trying to escape czarist Russia. My grandmother had silenced her daughter by clamping a hand over her mouth. One whimper and it was over. The pitchfork grazed the two-year-old's forehead."

Henry reacted with, "I know what you're getting at. We were already citizens."

I shut up. I didn't know that Henry, who had many faces, also had a sensitive side. Then Henry, trying to keep me awake, said that his Oregon teammates called him Cisco, a Mexican TV character of questionable intelligence. That told me that Oregon was like living in the 1930s and that minorities were an oddity. Although Henry laughed it off, I could tell it rubbed him the wrong way. *In high school, athletes joked about each other's heritage. But those teams were like family. Maybe Henry's teammates were all strangers. Not a good sign.*

* * *

JANUARY 6, 1958

UNIVERSITY OF OREGON

EUGENE, OREGON

The next day, Henry Ronquillo and I walked briskly down 13th Street, the business street that bisected the university. The sun was high overhead, and it was a damn 23 degrees—twenty degrees colder than I had ever experienced in Boyle Heights. Definitely not baseball weather for someone who had warm-weather dreams.

Since my knowledge of the university was limited, Henry had given me an orientation during the drive. My recruitment had only been a couple of telephone calls from the baseball coach and a couple of alumni, a thin brochure, and a couple of letters. In sum, Oregon was enthusiastic about my playing center field, school wouldn't cost me a dime, they would do anything to make me comfortable, and I fell for it.

* * *

I exhaled vapor as Henry and I walked past numerous retail shops as I tried to shake the kinks out of my legs from hours sitting behind the wheel, as well as sleeping in an uncomfortable bed in the sleeping porch at Henry's campus residence, the Philadelphia House, a Christian co-op.

Henry said. "I forgot to tell you. You're the first Jew who ever stepped foot in the house. But it doesn't matter now because classes won't begin for two days and the members won't start showing up until tonight. But you'll have to get your stuff out of there this afternoon."

I gave Henry a long look. "Anything else I should know?"

He giggled, and continued walking.

But the bed was free and I needed free.

Down the block, I received an odd look from a passing young lady in a windbreaker. *Am I out of place in my tweed overcoat, wool turtleneck, ski cap, and leather gloves? So damn cold here.* I glanced at Henry, a junior with dark eyes who could look right through you if he chose. He wore an unbuttoned green letterman's jacket, button-down shirt and beige cords. "You cold, Henry?"

"You'll get used to it."

We passed a row of brick-faced, one-story retail shops. Almost anything a student needed was there. Clothing. Typewriters. Dry cleaners. I braked at a bookstore and stared at textbooks and novels propped up in the windows thinking, *why isn't there a bookstore in Boyle Heights? In my house we only had library books. Good thing my textbook costs are covered here.*

When I turned away, I was drawn to a stack of newspapers in a metal kiosk near the curb. A front-page headline read: HUAC CALLS IN MORE HOLLYWOOD COMMIES.

As Henry approached, I pointed to the headline and rambled, "This is crazy, man! I know all about the Hollywood Communist Party. Robert Rossen, a distant cousin who won an Academy Award a few years ago, told my dad that when he came to Hollywood in the 1930s, actors, writers, directors, and producers who wanted to work in the movie industry had to attend communist get-togethers to be employed by the power players. Some joined the party. But they weren't a threat to overthrow the government. They just wanted a job. And the communist party has never been illegal."

"I watched the hearings," Henry said. "Rossen gave the committee 50 names of movie people. He put a lot of people out of work, out of the industry."

"Well, I wouldn't give them shit." I started walking down the street, Henry catching up to me.

"You'd go to jail."

"Yeah, I would . . . You can't put people in jail for the way they think."

"I'll visit you, man."

My stomach gurgled, letting me know I had to throw something down. I had eaten the last of Henry's burritos when we were a few hours out of Eugene. That's when Henry wolfed down my last salami sandwich. We had skipped breakfast to conserve funds. It was part of the "save your money, you never know what can happen to you" mentality in Boyle Heights. At my house we even saved paper clips.

At a stop light, looking up and down the street, I said, "Hey, let's get a burrito. There has to be a Mexican restaurant around here."

"This isn't Boyle Heights, man. 1958 hasn't come here yet. No rock and roll either. And they wouldn't know a Chicano if they saw one. This place is a goddamn 1948 Time Capsule."

We stopped briefly at a corner cafeteria and Henry said, "Follow me."

Thinking, *I'll eat anything that doesn't move*, I trailed Henry through double doors that kept the cold out. What a concept! Beyond the entrance, about a hundred noisy customers chowed down in the austere facility. I lined up behind Henry and a number of customers who edged their trays down an aluminum buffet counter to a wide variety of lunch offerings. The scent of hot soup and hot dogs filled the air and made my mouth water. I was thinking, *I could spare fifty cents for lunch*, when Henry said, "This is where our basketball team eats when school is out."

"So?"

"So you're Robbie Walters," Henry continued, as we approached a cart loaded with metal trays.

"I'm who?"

"When we get to the end of the line, sign your name Robbie Walters. He's a guard from Grant's Pass. He went home for break and won't be back until this afternoon. So you'll be him."

"How tall is Walters?"

"Six-two. But nobody knows him. He never plays. He's invisible."

"I got it." *At 5' 8" I'm the great imposter.* Apprehensive about my new identity, but starving, I piled four hot dogs and fries on my plate and mumbled, "Do they ever serve pastrami sandwiches?"

Annoyed with my question, Henry raised his voice. "I told you. Think 1948."

With my tray loaded up with hotdogs and fries, I reached the cashier's station. My eyes met the young lady's who stood patiently behind the cash register. Marilyn Monroe face, deep blue eyes, shoulder-length blonde hair. *She's got to be from general casting. Came to Hollywood to be an actress, didn't make it, drifted away.* I said nothing, and signed Walters on the Oregon Basketball clipboard. That was all I could remember.

The blonde read the clipboard upside down and asked, "Your first name. What's your first name?"

I turned to Henry, who waited for me at the end of the counter and asked sheepishly, "What's my first name?"

Henry said to the cashier, "Ever since Robbie's accident, he hasn't been himself."

I hurriedly scribbled "Robbie" on the clipboard and said to the cashier, "No, I'm not myself," then trailed Henry into the crowded room.

Henry made a beeline for a table on the far side of the room inhabited by two Black guys, the only Black people in the restaurant. They sat bolt upright and greeted Henry. I quickly joined Henry and his friends, who had crew cuts and were right out of Esquire with their Madras button-down shirts and newly pressed, flat-front khakis. Henry introduced me to Charlie Franklin, a guy with a stevedore build with long arms that could reach across the large red Formica table and touch its chrome rim. The other guy, Otis Davis, was long and trim, like a greyhound. I had noticed their names on the basketball list.

I met their inquisitive eyes as I slid my frame into a chair across from them.

"Burt is up from East Los Angeles College," Henry said. "We went there together. He was all-conference."

"How you guys doin'?" There was no response. Just looks. Not giving up on an icebreaker, I pointed at Charlie. "I remember you. You played at Manual Arts High, then L.A. City College."

Charlie deadpanned, "I like this guy. But does he have a hi-fi?"

My take: *Something in this guy is broken.* "Only a car radio," I responded.

Charlie continued, "But in summation, can he get my station?"

I took a sip of Coke. *Doesn't he ever stop?*

"Did you guys fly in?" Otis asked.

Charlie said, "Planes only take off from here. Nobody lands here."

I set my drink down and looked at Otis. The outside edges of his eyes had chicken marks. I guessed he was a few years older than Charlie, who would have been a twenty-two-year-old senior. I also inhaled the strong scent of after-shave lotion that seemed to be coming from Otis. He was Mr. Clean, like the TV commercial character.

Between bites of a hamburger, Otis said, "Must be like an oven in all those clothes."

I felt a drop of sweat edging its way down my forehead. Not wanting to be conspicuous, I wiped my forehead, and shoved the wool cap and gloves in my coat pocket and slipped off the overcoat.

"L.A., huh?" Otis said. "I played basketball at City College after Charlie. Then I came up here . . . So you got a full ride?"

"Room, board, books, tuition, and seventy-five bucks a month from a job—doing what, I don't know." While I shared a positive outlook, my mind drifted back to another recruitment meeting with baseball coach

Dutch Fehring at Stanford, when the coach told me that a scholarship was assured if I took two more community college classes. When I listened to Fehring, I recalled that he told the same thing to Ed Sadda, a great shortstop from San Diego City College. Then when Sadda showed up to campus, Fehring said he did not have a scholarship for him. Then next day, Sada signed for $60,000. I was no Sadda. And I didn't trust Fehring. I fiddled with my knife, turning it over, and said to Otis, "Where I come from, your word is your bond."

Henry set down his burger. "Because in Boyle Heights, if you break your word, they break your arm."

Otis finished his lunch, gave me a look. "I hope you're not going to write the book, *Sure Things*," suggesting I was too confident.

"He is a sure thing, man," Henry said, and raised his Coke. "I'm ready for the Bruins tonight. You guys ready?"

"Yeah," Charlie said. "UCLA is tough, but we think they're fluff. To keep them at bay, Coach Belko put in a play. I get the ball and they get small. Get my drift, sucka?"

Otis smiled at Charlie, and said, "*Game Plan*, by Charlie. It's not a bad book. His whole family bought one."

Charlie gave Otis a hard look. "And *Mouthing Off*, by Otis, may be a best seller."

After everyone finished eating, we walked four abreast down 13th street and entered a men's clothing store in the middle of the block. Near the entrance, I glanced at the merchandise and the prices. *Everything I want, nothing I can afford.*

Charlie strutted to the rear of the store and chatted with an older man who stood behind a counter packed with white dress shirts. The man gave Charlie a nod, walked to the sport shirt rack in the center of the store and pulled off three Madras shirts. He placed the items in a large paper bag and handed them to Charlie. No money was exchanged.

What the hell was that about? I thought.

A minute later, when we stood outside of the warm confines of the store, encouraging people to walk around us, Charlie said to us. "That guy loves me for some reason. Come on. I have to drop this off at my apartment."

We took off again toward campus and I put my hands deep into my pockets, trying to fend off the cold. That's when Henry said to me, "That was one of Charlie's sponsors."

I remembered my job at East L.A. Junior College, a campus largely of bungalows, with parking lots at both ends of the campus. The football coach, Clyde Johnson, who also served as assistant baseball coach, told me that my job would be working security in the parking lot from 6:00 to 10:00 p.m. "Report to Dave Holland," he said. "He's one of our linemen who supervises ten jocks that work security."

I reported for work that night and searched for Holland in both parking lots, but there was no sign of him or any security detail. After a lengthy search, I found Holland in the Student Union playing cards with a few other football guys. I said to him, "Coach Johnson told me to see you about the parking lot security job." Holland brought his cards to his chest, looked up and said, "You have a position, but no job." Then he continued playing, like that was my job orientation.

*   *   *

Crossing the street with our group, I said to Henry, "Tell me more about Oregon athletic sponsors."

"There are a lot of friends of the athletic department who take care of you because you're a star. I'm not a star. But Charlie's the man. Now we have to see if the university still loves Charlie after our 26 games are over."

Finish the season and you're not even a memory here? There's a lot more to that story.

Charlie did not comment and continued to strut down the street as if he owned the town. On the way, I glanced at passing students, all white. I thought, *Charlie, Otis, and Henry were the only people of color I had seen since I arrived in Eugene.* I didn't feel awkward. I was a minority, and came from, hung with, and played on multi-cultural teams . . . *Has the coach ever coached people of color before?. . . Does that make a difference?. . . Had there been people of color on the Oregon team before?. . . Was this new to the fans, and did it make a difference?*

Charlie's apartment was a sparsely furnished walk-up, above an ice-cream shop. It was dimly lit and had a kitchen, bedroom, and living room. I couldn't help but inhale the smell of dried sweat that appeared to be coming from a four-foot high pile of shirts and pants in the center of the living room.

In a near whisper, I asked Henry, "What's with the pile?"

Charlie said, "What's that, Ol' Fade?"

Henry said, "He means you're really Black, but your skin's faded."

I brushed it off, again asked, "So, what's with the pile?"

"I only wear these clothes once," Charlie said. "Then I go back and get some more."

I chuckled, "What are you going to do when the pile gets to the ceiling?"

"Throw them out, man. Don't you get it?"

I didn't get it. I kept my clothes in near perfect condition for a long time. But I felt good about knowing their secrets. Maybe I was accepted into the club. Or maybe they just didn't give a shit. One thing for sure, these guys were very entertaining.

Out of the blue, Otis pointed to a dent in the acoustical ceiling near the front door, about ten feet high, the height of a basketball rim. Suddenly, Otis sprung up and hammered his elbow to a tile, creating another dent, then landing with a thud. Charlie and Henry followed Otis, denting more tiles with their elbows.

Some kind of basketball macho thing.

They finished without saying a word and headed for the door.

I wondered what other eccentricities awaited me, and if "the man" was going to honor our verbal agreement.

Chapter 2

Later that afternoon, I drove a short distance to Roget Hall for my dorm room assignment. The two-story building was across the street from a grassy park, one block from the Student Union to the east and one block to the Physical Education building to the west. Its aged stone exterior was less inviting than the clean architectural lines I had seen at Stanford in August when they recruited me. No ivy growing up the walls. It was just plain old and unwelcoming. But it was a block away from the Student Union to the right, and the P.E. building to the left. At least they got that right.

I double-checked my map, felt confident I was at the right place, and marched upstairs with my arms loaded. It was as old inside as it was outside, and I had to walk sideways to avoid hitting the marred walls, or a flickering wall-sconce, with my broom and full-length mirror.

The dark mahogany door to my 10-by-15-foot room was open. Upon entering, I saw an Asian guy transferring items from his baggage on one of two desks to a tall cabinet. He was a few inches shorter than I, perhaps 5′5″. Growing up with a limited wardrobe, I believed that a well-dressed man indicated his wealth, so I was really into clothes. And I knew that his eyeglasses, pants, shirt, and shoes were of a foreign design not sold in Southern California. My immediate thought: *This should be interesting.*

He turned and appraised me. "Burt . . . Aki Tanaka from Japan . . . Your roommate." He laughed at the tail end of his sentence like we were stuck with each other. My sentiments exactly. He was from another planet, and we would have nothing in common. I was hoping to room with a jock, someone who was entertaining and a half-a-bubble off plum, like Henry. Not Charlie, who was a whole bubble off plum. And Otis? He was too conservative, but a very nice guy.

I placed a broom and mirror against the radiator pipes under the window that overlooked the park, then shook his hand. He pointed to the desk that his luggage was on and said, "I take this desk."

"Why'd you choose that one?"

"It's on the same side of the room as my couch."

There was a brief silence, as if we were two boxers circling each other in the ring, waiting a good moment to strike.

"Okay," I said, "I'll take the upper bunk in the sleeping porch."

"That room four bunk beds. I choose lower bunk."

"Aki, what made you choose Oregon?"

"Best marketing program. I have sponsor . . . Mr. Matsumoto. He sent me to learn best American methods of marketing manufactured product to sell in American."

I was a little hazy about the subject of marketing, but not about the fact that sub-standard Japanese products were the constant butt of jokes in southern California. "Made in Japan" meant the items were cheap and poorly crafted.

"What are you going to manufacture?"

"Automobiles."

Aki continued to unpack, and I thought, he's crazy. *Americans are not going to buy Japanese cars. General Motors and Ford will crush them.*

"But they hate you."

Aki spun around and said sharply, "I didn't bomb Pearl Harbor." There was silence for a long moment while he returned to unpacking. Then he asked, "Why you choose Oregon?"

"I have a baseball ride."

"A ride?"

"A scholarship."

We eyed each other, then Aki asked, "Why you have mirror and broom?"

"It's to improve my baseball swing. I practice swinging the broom in front of the mirror. I watch my swing and make sure it's perfect."

His eyebrows furrowed. "You need larger room."

* * *

At 7 p.m. that night, I arrived at MacArthur Court for the UCLA game and watched Henry, Charlie, and Otis perform. Although registration for classes was two days away, the 9,500-seat arena was almost packed with students. From my seat at floor level, several thousand noisy fans seemed to hang over the court from the balconies 70 to 80 feet above me. I was impressed. This was big-time basketball compared to games at the Pan Pacific Auditorium in West Los Angeles where 6,600 fans packed temporary bleachers for a Bruins or Trojans game.

I had been thinking lately about becoming a coach after my playing career. I had limited knowledge of the game of basketball and knew I had a long way to go before I was competent in that sport. So I watched the UCLA game with great interest, hoping to pick up a coaching point or two. I shifted on the hard bench seat to get comfortable, then thought about the few players of color I had watched when UCLA played USC. *The Bruins had one Black player, All-American Walt Torrance, and had had several outstanding Black players in the previous six seasons. USC, considered a racist school in Boyle Heights, had one Black basketball player. But that guy's name and number were never in the program. In other words, you would see him playing, but for the benefit of the alumni, he wasn't really there. Then there was the case of a good friend of mine, an All L.A. City player, Kaz Shinzato, from my high school. Kaz had a basketball scholarship at SC, but they never played him at home. I suspected that it would have been an affront to the racist alumni if they saw Kaz, a Japanese-American, in a Trojan uniform.*

My mind returned to the game, and the only thing I learned was that

Otis Davis had unbelievable spring in a pre-game layup drill. I guessed he had the lift of about 48 inches before he dropped the ball into the rim. *This guy could be a high jumper*, I thought.

As Charlie Franklin intimated earlier, there were special plays to get him the ball down low, where he scored 20 points. But he didn't score enough, and Oregon lost by five in a game where Otis and Henry played only one minute.

At game's end, as I stood with the rest of the students and listened to the band across the court play the alma mater, a middle-aged man in a dark green sweater-shirt and brown slacks approached me. He said over the music, "Are you Burt Golden?"

"Yes." I was amazed that he would know who I was.

"Your L.A. letterman's jacket is a dead giveaway. I'm Don Kirsch, the baseball coach."

We shook hands and I waited for him to say something positive. But Kirsch who had awarded me a scholarship over the phone now had concern in his voice and on his face. I thought, *maybe he's had a tough day*.

"Come to my office," he said. "It's a short walk."

Not the words of welcome I hoped for.

During our walk down the long arena hallway to a connecting building, he didn't say much and I thought he was an introvert. Finally, we entered a small office with a smattering of team photos on the walls. I took a seat across from him and wondered where my photo would go.

"I have something to tell you," Kirsch said in a somber tone.

Uh-oh. Something's not right.

"The center fielder I thought was going to sign with the Yankees is returning. He's been on scholarship for three years. I have to give him his fourth year."

Emotion welled up inside me and came to the surface in the form of anger. "Wait a second! Are you saying I *had* his scholarship?" I shook my head in disbelief. "No! You're kidding. I was awarded a scholarship. I had your word. The athletic department already paid for my room. You can't do what I think you're doing."

"Things were in motion," Kirsch said. "I thought you were in, but you're not. You can keep the room for the quarter, but I can't give you meals, tuition, or books. I'm sorry."

"I came a thousand miles for this? I turned down Iowa and San Jose State after being admitted to come here." *If I didn't get sick last October I'd be at Cal.* "I can't believe you just moved a guy in front of me at my position. Now my back is to the wall. If I register for classes and don't play I lose a year of eligibility. According to the NCAA, I have five years to play four seasons. I've already played two seasons. If I transfer to another university in the conference, I lose a year of eligibility because of a conference transfer rule . . . I'm a damn good player-all-conference. I don't believe this. Last month you thought I would be a starter."

Kirsch ran a hand across his face. "I'll tell you what. Come out for the team. If you beat this guy out, I'll personally pay for your next quarter. Right now, I don't have the funds."

In other words, "your dream isn't worth a shit." I sprung from my chair and walked out, slamming the door behind me. Down the hall I marched, not knowing whether to shit or go blind. Outside it was cold and dark. I jaywalked across the street to a small park where I stood under a broken street lamp, my head down, trying to get my bearings. I buttoned up my jacket, slid my hands deep into my pockets and exhaled vapor. Nothing made sense. I stared into the unknown and thought, *who does he think he is, screwing me like that? But I have no contract.* I thought about my girlfriend, Joan Orshoff, back home. Good looking, smart, genuine, she was like the first cup of coffee in the morning. I inhaled the frozen north, and remembered her mother telling me, "If you go to Oregon, your relationship with my daughter will be over." *Boy, are you fucked up! . . . But every university that wanted me was out of L.A . . . Baseball is everything . . . That's why I'm here . . . No, you're not here. You're not anywhere . . . Screw the odds makers . . . Son of a bitch. You're not going home a failure.*

I watched a couple of guys coming out of Mac Court across the street. *They have a place to go. I'm lost. I can transfer and wait out a year before I'm eligible at another university. No. I would be too old to sign with a major league team, pay my dues in minors and work my way up to the majors. Develop your skills. That's why you're here.*

I've come back before. Life-threatening spinal injury in high school to leading Los Angeles schools in home runs, then making all-junior college. Three years ago the doctor told you physical contact could cause paralysis . . . Funny how you learned to hide injuries. In Boyle Heights, players would laugh at you if you were injured. Worse if you complained. Kirsch has no idea . . . You've made it this far without being in a wheelchair . . . But, no money, no school, no baseball . . . There's a solution. But everything has to fall into place.

I ran back to Kirsch's office, hoping he was still there. Winded, I entered and blurted, "You've already paid for my dorm room." Kirsch looked up from some paperwork, wide-eyed, like he thought he would never see me again. "How about getting me a job to pay for my meals?"

He hesitated for a long moment, thawed, and said, "I'll get you a job serving food and washing pots and pans in your dorm cafeteria. It'll pay half of what the scholarship athletes are paid—75 cents an hour. But you'll eat."

As he spoke, I went over in my mind my new plan: *Walk-on and earn a scholarship in the spring quarter. Sign a baseball contract in two years. Now I have to pay for tuition and books with the cash buried in a tennis ball can in the trunk of my car. That would clean me out. But I'll figure something else out.*

Minutes later, inside a wood framed payphone booth in the dimly lit hallway of the empty arena, I took a deep breath and called home. *If my father answered I would tell him the truth. He would call me crazy— his standard evaluation of me. He would say, "You should have gone to Stanford or Cal." And I would have to remind him that I was in bed for six weeks last fall with the Asian flu and had to drop the classes I needed to transfer.* My father didn't think he had choices and he tried to sell that attitude to me.

Coming out of Boyle Heights, I thought I had choices, that my world wasn't limited. But I did not know the price I would have to pay to acquire my choices.

My father answered. I lied and told him everything was great and paid for, that I got a great job supervising the dorm cafeteria. He was pleased. And I didn't receive his favorite derogatory comment.

After I hung up, I went downstairs and caught Henry coming out of the locker room. We talked Oregon basketball as we walked down a darkened street to the Student Union where I explained my status at the university.

In the middle of the union, surrounded by night-owl students who probably came from the game to wolf down another meal, we sipped five-cent tea, the only thing we could afford. Henry glanced at the skirts coming and going, then waved a hand in my direction and spoke over the chatter. "You can't go back to your part-time playground director job in Boyle Heights. One night you'd be ice-picked to death like the guy you replaced."

"That was a bad night job," I said. "I couldn't study when a gang drove by and riddled the swimming pool walls with gunfire. Did I ever tell you? . . . A couple of rounds came close to my window." I chuckled. "That shit used to break my concentration. Do you know about the over-dosed hood I found unconscious in the ball closet? . . . No. I'm not going back to that shit. I just have to make it to spring quarter."

Chapter 3

Dampened by a cold Oregon mist, wishing for a sunny southern California day, I walked quickly to the P.E. building from my dorm for my first class. I had ten dollars left after paying for tuition and a couple of texts and I figured it could buy a lot of tea, one long distance phone call, or at 23 cents a gallon of gas, a trip to San Francisco in my car. Then I thought, *what I feared most growing up was poverty . . . I'm at the base of Maslow's Pyramid: food, shelter and clothing . . . Who the fuck was Maslow, anyway? He probably couldn't hit the curve.*

Doing my best to maintain my balance while crossing the slippery street with my leather soles, I thought, *I've been there. Got a full-time job at 15. Worked all summer. Made enough to buy an oven for Mom and some clothes for me . . . Son of a bitch! Just keep going. Something good is going to happen.*

There was one chair open in the History of Physical Education class. About forty students in wet, foul-weather attire lent to the room's dank smell. I slid into the seat, set my notebook on the desk, sat back and awaited the professor. *You're doing the right thing . . . a physical education major will insure a public school paycheck every month after your baseball career. Can't be like dad. Commission sales. Selling furniture and appliances door-to-door in the toughest areas of Los Angeles. Living hand-to-mouth . . . How the hell does he do that? Day-after-day?*

Week-after-week?

Otis Davis sat quietly to my left. I was right behind a blonde guy wearing a green Oregon letterman's jacket. I placed my notebook, two texts, and *The Art of War* on my desk. I had picked up that book in Los Angeles and believed that there were strategies written by Sun Tzu in 512 B.C. that could help me become a good coach.

Seeking to meet new people, I tapped the blonde guy who sat in front of me on the shoulder. "Excuse me," I said. "Did you go to the Rose Bowl game?"

His head swiveled back and he looked at me with contempt. "I was the quarterback," he said, as if he was royalty and I was a peasant.

Asshole! No wonder Oregon lost.

Just then, the professor, Dr. Sigerseth, entered and lumbered to the head of the classroom. He was formally dressed, a tall man with sparse gray hair and slumped shoulders. Listening to a few formalities, I wondered if he had ever played ball and how he got to be in front of us. That thought left quickly when he began his lecture on how American physical education evolved from Swedish and German gymnastics. While taking copious notes I wondered, *how many more of his boring lectures do I have to live through? Is this the price of success?*

I listened closely to Sigerseth, but didn't pick up anything that I could earn a living with. Halfway through the lecture, I glanced at Otis. He was scratching out notes in between making a number of hash marks at the top of his paper. Then something echoed in my brain as Sigerseth said, *"These are the kinds of things* that you will be learning here this quarter." He had repeated the phrase "these are the kinds of things" so many times he had worn it out.

"Otis," I whispered. "What are those marks on the top of your paper for?"

"That's the number of times Sigerseth said, 'these are the kinds of things' today. He's got 20. His record is 25."

I nodded. *Next time I'll keep track.*

When class was dismissed, I headed to the door, hoping my next class would be of some monetary value. That's when Sigerseth called out, "Mr. Golden, may I see you?"

I turned back, astonished that he knew my name since he didn't take roll. He approached with, "Coach Kirsch called me this morning. He said look for a guy in an L.A. letterman's jacket and good tan. He's one of ours." The professor placed a hand on my shoulder. "What I want you to know is we take care of our jocks, but you have to attend class."

These are the kinds of things that will keep me eligible.

I thanked him. Although I disliked most of my lower-division classes, I never missed one class. But it was nice for Kirsch to call.

Sigerseth walked with me down the hallway, full of students traveling in every direction. "By the way," he said, "Do you know Charlie Franklin? He's also from L.A."

"We've met."

"Charlie signed up for my class, but he was absent today. If you see him, tell him he must attend class or I will drop him."

Sigerseth doesn't have much faith in Charlie making an appearance.

* * *

Fired up to be on time for Educational Psychology, I jogged to class through the cemetery across the street that was slotted with deteriorated tombstones, my shoes tamping down wet pine needles from overhanging tree branches. I passed many students who walked leisurely in the same direction, and I wondered why I was the only one running.

I entered a classroom three times as large as Sigerseth's room and took a seat across from Otis Davis up front. We talked basketball for five, then ten, then fifteen minutes. No professor. Eventually, all the chairs were taken, and I sensed that almost everyone knew there was no hurry getting to this class. Finally, the professor arrived, said nothing about his tardiness, didn't give his name, didn't take roll, and began to scratch out educational statistics on the large chalkboard on a sidewall, over and over again, down the board.

The guy is a stat freak, in another world. I'm seeking behavioral science information.

I didn't take any notes, thinking he couldn't possibly test on this minutia. But Otis was copying everything. He was like a windup student. Sit him down in classroom and he suddenly becomes operational.

I was greatly interested in the psychology of the learning process, and hoped for a piece of wisdom, like the comment L.A. Dodger general manager Al Campanis had said in the *L.A. Times* recently. Tuning out the professor, I tried to remember what Campanis said. Then it came to me: "*If a player isn't responding to coaching, it's because he doesn't understand it, can't do it, or doesn't want to do it. It's our job to figure out which one when working with him.*" Stuff like that turned me on.

The professor continued to note irrelevant statistics, and he was driving me crazy.

Disgruntled, I read a strategy from *The Art of War*. "*If you know the enemy and know yourself, you may not fear the result of a hundred battles.*" My interpretation: *Since I didn't know where the professor was going, and didn't know myself very well, I was in trouble.*

Not having an immediate answer to a forthcoming course problem, I let it rest while I exercised my eyes to improve my hitting reaction by dancing my eyes from one corner of the room to the other as quickly as I could. My eyes jogged up and down cabinets, across the professor's desk and back. After ten minutes I stopped and thought, *can I do this for two years? Is this the price of a degree and a ticket to a steady job? Sun Tzu said victory is reserved for those willing to pay the price. But learning what the hell the price is continues to be such a mystery.*

Toward the end of the hour the professor told us that we needed to purchase an additional text, *Modern Educational Psychology*. "Nine dollars." Sitting there, still awake, I thought, *skip the book, save your money for an emergency and somehow pass this class.*

Seconds later, while continuing on his statistical rampage, the professor's eyes suddenly closed and his writing hand slowly drifted down the chalkboard scraping the board with a scraggly line. He stood there, immobile, like he was sleeping. Students glanced at each other, waited for the professor to come back. Minutes went by, and then one-by-one the students quietly left the room.

Otis said to me in a hushed voice, "It's his malaria drugs. Let's go"
"When will he wake up?"
"Don't worry, man. Let's go."

Chapter 4

I registered for Wrestling Methods, Boxing Methods, and Baseball Conditioning to get me in the best shape of my life and beat out the guy who took my scholarship. That gave me three hours of workouts after lunch. A plausible idea, since I thought that I had totally recovered from the Asian flu that had killed 160,000 nationally. But I had no idea that boxing workouts would demand all the endurance I could muster, and that because of those consecutive workouts I would be totally drained after three hours.

After enduring an hour of wrestling, I lined up with my back to the boxing ring wearing the P.E. uniform, white shorts and T-shirt, with 20 other jocks from different athletic teams. The instructor, a middle-aged man of average size, went down our row and asked us about our fighting experience.

He asked the muscular Hawaiian guy next to me, who I guessed was in my weight class (160-165 pounds). Then I heard, "I'm CYO (Catholic Youth Organization) champion of Hawaii."

Oh, shit! That's like being a pro . . . And I have to fight him.

The instructor, who hadn't called roll, and didn't know our names, pointed at me. "What kind of fight experience have you had?"

When I hesitated, he said sharply, "Out with it! Your experience!"

"Brawls, sir."

There was sporadic laughter.

The instructor stared me down. "Can you be more explicit?"

"I fought in brawls on the athletic field."

"Did you win?"

"No winners, sir. They were all broken up."

"There will be no bare-knuckle fights here," the instructor said. "You will wear headgear and 16-ounce gloves, as opposed to the 8-ounce gloves the pros wear. And you will fight every day. Every day you will fight," he repeated, as if he thought we didn't hear him.

The son of a bitch is training us to parachute behind enemy lines.

At a trim 6′2″, Otis Davis was next in line and said that he had no previous boxing experience. And added, "But it looks like fun."

"Then you fight that guy," I said to him, pointing to Hawaiian guy.

"No, thanks," Otis said in a hushed voice.

Standing next to Otis was George Padovan, a giddy 6′4″ basketballer, who joked and poked Otis. Otis had introduced me to Padovan. Padovan was from San Pedro, a tough port town in Los Angeles, and was missing a front tooth, maybe from one of the bar fights he proudly told the instructor about.

Next to Padovan was Bob Heard, a defensive tackle on the football team, whose frame could block the sun. His sour, dark face indicated that he never met a man he liked. He grunted in response to the experience question. "Yeah, I fought."

* * *

By four o'clock, I had wrestled, boxed, and lifted weights with the baseball team. And I was exhausted. But I dragged myself and my full-length mirror and broom downstairs in Mac Court to the basketball locker room. *If Ted Williams, the great Red Sox hitter, swung in front of a mirror, so could I. It makes complete sense to me.*

In the locker room, the lighting was decent, the room cold, and the door open. I knew it was out-of-bounds for anyone not on the basketball team, but "what the hell." *It was dry and I had friends.*

A marred coffee table was in the corner, several yards from two walls of tall, gray metal lockers. I placed my five-foot tall mirror upright against a table, and practiced my swing without any intrusions. Basketball practice was being conducted upstairs and I knew I had to get out when the thunderous sound of players running and jumping above the ceiling stopped, because the players would be returning to the locker room.

After about ten minutes, my hands began to blister. Then the ceiling noise stopped, and in seconds I heard players rambling down the nearby wood staircase. For some reason, I kept swinging in front of the mirror, focusing on attacking mythical pitches in my strike zone. I tried to ignore the players, but finally caught their glare. And gave them a look, like I belonged there. Sweat dripped profusely from their heads to their chests, drenching cotton T-shirts that clung to their bodies like wet paper. And as they stripped down to take a shower, the stink from sweaty socks and shoes, as well as the scent of wintergreen from the analgesic Ben Gay, took over the room.

I swung the broom for a few more minutes. There I was. Twelve naked men, me and a broom.

Henry came over. Soaked with sweat, he said in a somber tone, "Burt, you can practice down here until Coach Belko says something. I don't know how he's going to feel about this. But if he says something to me I'll let you know." He pointed back to George Padovan who was slipping off his jock. "This is George Padovan. He's from L.A. San Pedro." I had trouble shaking hands with nude men, so I nodded, and said, "We met in boxing class."

"Yeah," Padovan said, "You're the baseball guy."

"Baseball doesn't start up for a month because of the rain, so I'm practicing my swing."

Padovan shot me a grin. "This ain't S.P., Jack."

My interpretation: *He was defining Oregon. The people, the food, the weather. And he means S.P. as in San Pedro, not the Southern Pacific Railway.*

The broom still in my hand, I walked over to Charlie Franklin, who had his locker next to Otis. He was heading for the shower. "Charlie," I called out, "Professor Sigerseth asked about you this morning."

Charlie looked straight ahead. "Don't worry about Charlie," adding to the mystery of his existence at the university.

Otis, on his way to the shower, said to me, "*Education,* by Charlie, a bad book."

I returned to swinging my broom in the far corner of the room, unconcerned about Charlie, since he wasn't worried about himself. Soon the blister on my palm began to bleed. While studying the extent of my injury, I saw someone walking toward me. I looked over. It was the man, Coach Belko, in a green jacket and pants. About 5'9", he stared coldly at me. And I knew I had crossed the border, invaded Oregon nation.

"What the hell are you doing?" He took a drag on his pipe and waited patiently for me to respond.

"I'm Burt Golden. I'm Henry's friend. Just transferred in from East L.A. JC. I'm going to play baseball and I'm just practicing my swing."

Belko twisted his face and walked away.

I wondered if his retreat meant I could return to the locker room, or he was trying to figure out what the hell to do with me.

Chapter 5

The next morning, wanting to look like other jocks, I got a crew cut in the training room that was adjacent to the basketball locker room. An offensive lineman, who used electric shears that also shaved ankles before they were taped, turned barber for two bucks. He was quick and accurate, and there was a line of waiting jocks across the room. Now all I had in my tennis ball can was eight bucks, enough for 32 hot dogs, or a long-distance call to my parents telling them how wonderful things were.

* * *

That afternoon, I showed up to baseball conditioning in the dusty hallway of Mac Court with my new look. Somehow the other outfielders knew where I came from and that I wanted their job and their scholarship. They acted like I had the plague. Froze me out of conversations. And Coach Kirsch made no effort to create camaraderie within the group. Not even an introduction.

We divided up by position to run 40-yard sprints in the hallway. My sense was that Coach wanted to get us in shape and keep us busy since we couldn't play outside for months. I ran with eight other outfielders, knowing that only four of us were going to make the team. I came in first in all sprints, but as fast as I ran, I only got a nod from Coach Kirsch.

After the tedious hour-long baseball workout, I was exhausted. And I literally dragged myself upstairs in the arena to watch my basketball friends go through their paces. I sat there trying to recover, hoping to pick up some coaching pointers.

Coach Belko, wearing green sweats, walked five players through a new play. A few minutes later, this group of two white guys plus Charlie, Otis and Henry, went full speed, cutting every which way at half court. Shoes squeaked, arms and legs moved like engine pistons. Belko, standing at mid-court, hands on hips, suddenly screamed, "No, Otis. You're in the wrong place." Players froze as Belko pointed across the court where Charlie stood, chest out, in the low post. "Otis, you're supposed to be over there. It's a double screen."

"Oh, shoot," Otis mumbled as he eyed the floor.

From what I had seen, Belko ran a series of plays, difficult to remember unless there was a lot of repetition, which apparently they didn't have enough of. Although the other players accurately followed direction, I thought Belko was asking too much.

When they ran the play again, Belko stopped the motion again by blowing his whistle and yelling, "Otis, pay attention. There are two screens, not one." Again Otis hung his head.

If Belko can't trust him, he's not going to play.

Finally, they went full court, five-on-five, running the play that was just installed. The second time down court, the wiry Henry set an illegal screen, crashing into his smaller defender, knocking him off balance. That player responded with a forearm to Henry's chin. I leaned forward and wondered which Henry would react—the guy who was dancing through life, or the East L.A. guy who was meaner than a junkyard dog.

Henry recovered, glared at this defender; his short fuse ignited the killer side of his brain. He shot a right cross, made contact with a glass jaw, sending the other guy to the floor. Players rushed over and pulled Henry back. His opponent remained on the floor face up, immobile, looking like a jigsaw puzzle with a couple of pieces gone.

There was dead silence as the players who gathered around the fight site eyed Belko. It was his move.

Belko yelled, "Damn it, Henry! Aren't you ever going to learn? Get out of here. Shower up."

This wasn't Henry's first fight. And it wouldn't be his last.

Fights were commonplace on court during basketball practice at our high school. *You were defending your honor. Whatever that was, I never figured out.* Now Belko had to restrain Henry's raw instincts and teach him that losing his head would result in a technical foul, getting thrown out of the game, and change the momentum of the contest. He had to get East L.A. out of his system.

I showered, then hustled to the basketball locker room just as practice ended. I had left my broom and mirror leaning against a far wall, and thought I could get in some swings when the team was showering and wanted to see how Belko was going to handle Henry.

In my mirror, I saw Belko follow the players into the room, talk quietly to Henry for a few minutes, then stood in the corner smoking his pipe and eyeing me. That wasn't good. He slid the pipe out of his mouth and returned to Henry, who was tying his shoes. I couldn't hear what was said, but I could see how tight Belko's face was. I thought he was counseling Henry.

I assumed my hitting stance and prepared to swing when Henry appeared, almost becoming the victim of my broom head. I held up, and listened to him say, "Burt, Belko just talked with me. He said, 'I don't care if Burt is a nice guy, he's going to have to get his mirror and that fuckin' broom the hell out of here.'"

I nodded in agreement. *I can see Coach's point. I don't belong here. But I'll be back.*

Chapter 6

Wondering how Henry and Belko were going to survive each other, I met Henry in the Jazz Room of the Student Union after dinner. This was a little-known place of refuge where normal people showed up from time to time. There were five soft chairs in a gray-walled room the size of a one-car garage. In one corner stood a large hi-fi cabinet. I noticed that records were checked out and stored in a small adjacent room. It was a place where you could relax, listen to the music of the day and focus on a little homework.

Henry was studying notes in his three-ring binder. I took a seat to his left, wearing a gray, zipped up wool car coat. I was always cold. Said nothing and began to acquaint myself with a chapter for Sigerseth's class. We were the only two students in the room. The Belko update would have to wait.

Within a minute, Henry pointed at a guy apparently taking inventory in the storage room directly in front of us. Henry didn't tell me what he was thinking, I didn't ask, but I was curious. I listened to Elvis Presley sing, "I walk alone," which could have been my theme song. My mind wandered, as it often did when I read, and I said to Henry, "How old is Otis?"

"He's twenty-seven. He was in the Air Force five years."

"Was he a pilot?"

"No. He played basketball for Special Services. That's an entertainment branch of the military."

"What a gig."

"You got it."

One question led to another. "Counting two years in junior college, probably three in high school and five in the Air Force, he's played basketball for ten years. So why doesn't he get Belko's offense?"

Henry flicked his hand. "Because this is his first experience in a structured offense."

"He's in trouble," I said. "I heard Belko yelling at him today. I hope that doesn't hurt Otis's playing time."

Just then, Otis and George Padovan strolled in, ending our conversation. Although it was 40 degrees outside, Otis, who always looked like he came out of GQ, wore a beige, V-neck sweater over a white T-shirt, and Padovan wore his blue Harbor Junior College State Champions jacket over a white T-shirt. Style of the day.

They took seats across from Henry and me and quickly evaluated their workout performance by needling each other with the names of hypothetical books supposedly written by the player with a particular issue.

Padovan, exposed a limited set of teeth as he said, "*How to Survive Coaching*, by Ronquillo, with a preface by Otis."

Otis followed up with, "*Getting on the Coach's Good Side*, by Ronquillo."

Henry raised his voice as he pointed at Otis. "Robbie clipped me. He deserved it."

"Oh, yeah," Otis said. "You're from L.A. and Robbie is from Oregon. Oregon players have a special dispensation."

"You don't even know what the fuck 'dispensation' means," Henry countered.

Otis responded, "It means you can get away with shit. That's what it means."

Suddenly conversation stopped as the guy with glasses in the storage room stepped out and disappeared into the hallway. Henry watched the

36

guy all the way, sprung from his chair and gave Otis the thumbs-up.

Otis's eyes widened. "Oh, no," he said with a sense of urgency and quickly exited the room.

Something's going down. Otis has seen this act and is a clean machine.

Padovan got up and covered the hallway as I watched Henry enter the storage room, remove a 78 long play from a slot in the storage room, then slide the black disc down the backside of his pants, under his letterman jacket. Looking nonchalant, he walked out of the Jazz Room singing Sinatra lyrics, "That's why the lady is tramp."

Henry and Padovan are willing to risk their scholarship and their reputation for a four-dollar record.

When Henry was halfway out the door, I shot out of my seat, headed for the dorm thinking: *How big is Henry's collection? And how many times could I be an innocent bystander before being implicated?*

Chapter 7

The following week, a headline in the student newspaper said, "Not Expecting Rain? You're Not in Eugene." It was enough to make me think that I would never see sun again.

It had been raining for 14 straight days when I entered boxing class to go head-to-head with the CYO Boxing Champion of Hawaii. All the jocks dressed to maul each other in whites, surrounded the ring and took bets on my survival. I overheard someone saying that I was favored to go down in the three-round match. My strategy: Stay away from the guy.

Reluctantly, I met Hawaiian guy in the middle of the ring, and we touched gloves to begin the first round. I backed up. He closed in. Then, I didn't see the punch coming that riveted my mouth guard. That was followed by another punch that knocked my head from one side to the other. Still knowing where I was, I circled him, hoping that he couldn't hit a moving target. Wrong again. I fielded a barrage of blows to my headgear and I mistakenly danced myself into the ropes, throwing a number of left hooks and jabs on the way. But he blocked all my punches, like he knew what was coming. Not a confidence builder for me.

On the ropes, I kept swinging, hoping something would land. After using up my energy dancing on the canvas in the toe-to-toe battle, fatigue set in. My gloved hands suddenly felt like hundred-pound weights, and they dropped from protecting my head to my waist. I became a human punching bag for Hawaiian guy, while I waited in pain for the bell to ring ending the three-minute round.

Those that bet on my survival yelled, "Get your gloves up."

But I did not respond. I couldn't. My arms suddenly weighed a ton. All I could do was wait for the bell. The slowest three-minutes of my life. Time stood still while I moved my head from side-to-side, trying to stay alive, and thinking, *why did I sign up for this damn class?*

Finally, the bell rang and I staggered to my corner, receiving cheers from those who bet on me to survive the first round.

After a brief rest, I regained enough energy to hold my gloves up again, this time with a survival plan. We met in the center of the ring, and I immediately wrapped my gloves and arms around his, preventing him from throwing a punch. When he pushed my gloves away, I moved in on him and did it again. Hawaiian guy was in a tangled web, my only defense. I continued this unorthodox style until the bell rang.

We clinched during most of the third round, and the bell rang ending the bout. *No way I can wear myself out and play baseball. Drop the class . . . No. You're not a quitter.*

Arguing with myself, and feeling like I had just run a marathon, I was overjoyed that baseball workout was cancelled that day. My weight was down from 162 to 159, and I wondered if I had misunderstood a Sun Tzu's war theory, *He who wishes to fight must first count the cost.*

* * *

That afternoon, Henry asked me if I would drive Charlie, Otis, and him to a dentist's office. The dentist was going to pay Charlie for "assisting him"—a clear violation of the "no money under the table" NCAA rule. Interested to see the payoff, I agreed. Charlie was supposed to receive $300 for six hours of work. The dentist had told Charlie it would take six trips to his office for full payment.

As the elevator shot us up to the second floor of the downtown low-rise medical building, a red-headed woman in our compartment was serenaded by Charlie, who gave her an engaging smile and sang, "You for me, and me for you, together."

It was Charlie's specialty, making people feel uncomfortable. And he certainly succeeded, for I felt awkward as hell. And there was the woman, stuck in the elevator with some guy who probably just escaped the home.

On the second floor, Charlie, in green Oregon warm-ups, led us into the dentist's reception area, eight wing chairs and a counter. Before sitting down, Henry said to me in a low tone, "Charlie sang to Coach Belko's wife when Coach drove us to see an Oregon State game at Corvallis a couple of months ago."

I shook my head, and wondered what Charlie was going to do next.

As we waited in the packed room, I read a short story in a *Photoplay* magazine about Liz Taylor's third husband dying in a plane crash. I was a big movie fan with no money to go to the movies and Liz Taylor was the number one entertainment attraction.

Suddenly, Charlie emerged from the back office all smiles, like he had just won an Academy Award. He strutted toward us with an ear-to-ear grin. "Let's go," he said to his entourage.

In the hallway, Charlie leaped up about ten feet and dented a ceiling acoustical tile with his elbow. Henry and Otis followed, no doubt punctuating their visit.

"What did he pay you?" I asked Charlie.

"I took $300 and squared account. That's twelve hundred an hour. And that's what I'm worth."

I pressed the elevator button, as Henry said, "Until the 26 games are over."

"Don't worry about Charlie," Charlie said.

Charlie's ego has an ego, I thought.

As for me, I was making real progress. In a short time, I had lost my scholarship, got beaten up in class, could have been considered a co-conspirator in a theft, and was privy to a pay-off.

Chapter 8

The University of Idaho's basketball team came to town in late January, and my basketball friends were really looking forward to the game. Idaho was in last place, which meant that Oregon was probably going to jump out to an early lead and Henry, Otis, and Padovan would get more playing time.

I slipped into the basketball locker room well before game time to see the L.A. contingent. The room was super quiet as the players dressed for the game. Several of them gave me the evil eye, but said nothing. I was there because I had nothing else to do with my life. And Belko wasn't there to throw me out.

Standing in the center of the room, I turned to hear Padovan in a far corner calling, "Hey, Henry," like he was hailing a taxi. Padovan held up a pair of beige sweat socks with enthusiasm. "Look at this. They ran the dryer too long and burnt the socks. Just the right color for our khakis."

I thought, *with the $15 a month spending money they're allowed, everything counts.*

As Henry slipped on his jock he shot back, "I don't have room in my sock drawer."

I remembered that Henry had shown me a dresser drawer full of athletic department sweat socks. And I wondered what else he had liberated.

Just then the manager, a short bespectacled guy, walked over to half-dressed Charlie, as if he was subservient to the star, and held out four game tickets. "This is for tonight's game."

"What am I going to do with them, man?" Charlie responded.

"All I do is hand them out."

Charlie shook his head and placed the tickets on the top shelf of his gray metal locker, as did the other players who received their ticket allotment.

Tickets! Money! Could be my Sunday meals when the cafeteria is closed for lunch and dinner. Sell the tickets. Split the profits with the players. Not now, but soon.

Reserving that thought for the right time, I found Otis on the other side of the room, sitting on a bench, next to a guy taking his pulse with an index finger while holding a stopwatch in the other hand. I introduced myself to Mark Elliot, a master's degree student. He was recording the pulse and blood pressure of athletes before and after their activity for his thesis. Elliot was trim, had a baby face and a friendly manner. Curious, I took a seat next to him and asked, "How are Otis's numbers?"

Elliot gave me a slow disbelieving headshake. "This is the second time I've tested him. His pulse doesn't change. It's low before a game. It's low right after the game. It's so low he could fall asleep on the court."

Otis chuckled, "That's what Belko told me."

"Are you out for a sport?" Elliot asked me.

"Baseball."

"Are you quick?"

"Very."

"Hey," he said with enthusiasm, "I've got another study. I'm comparing the quickest Oregon athletes in different sports. I've tested guys from basketball, football, track, and tennis and I still need a quick baseball player."

"Count me in."

"Okay. Meet me in the gymnastics room. Monday, 10 a.m. That's just down the hall from the P.E. administrative office. Wear shorts and shoes."

*   *   *

After the Idaho game, which Oregon won easily, Carl Taylor, a wide-body 5′8″ met our L.A. contingent in the dressing room. Carl was balding and maybe 30 years old. I listened to him tell our group what great players they were. I had learned that Carl wasn't married and didn't seem to have a life other than his dry cleaning business and was somehow connected to my friends. He invited the guys out for a late dinner. For reasons that I would soon understand, I was also invited.

It was raining as Carl drove us across town on crowned streets to a restaurant that was still open at 10 p.m. A few other low-rise businesses down the dimly lit block were already dark. I figured that the crowned streets were needed for water run-off in a state where the rain never stopped. It was our thirtieth straight wet day. And I was tired of counting.

Inside the empty restaurant it was so cold we had to keep our jackets on. We took seats at a long, highly glossed picnic table that had a shiny bronze metal lamp hanging down at eye level and ordered. In no time, the casually dressed waiter brought each of us a hamburger and drinks. Between bites, Padovan lit up a cigarette and took a long drag.

Otis, sitting across from him, said, "Those things got you in trouble."

Padovan eyed his accuser. "So I lit up when we got off the bus to Denver Arena. So fuckin' what? I've been smoking since I was 13."

"Yeah, but you didn't put it out when Coach asked you to."

Padovan's eyes sharpened. He held out the cigarette like he didn't give a damn. Then he took another drag. "I told Belko I'm a smoker. Navy guys smoke, man."

Carl reacted by pulling out a pack of unfiltered Chesterfields from his shirt pocket and placing them in the middle of the table, like he was sharing, or it was his way of saying, "I'm with you Padovan." No one else smoked, and Carl waited until dessert was served to light up. As his smoke engulfed the low-hanging bronze lamp, Carl challenged our egos with, "Who's the fastest runner at this table?"

Charlie, sitting as straight as a board, confidently said, "That's my meat. I used to run track."

Henry said, "You're overrated, Charlie. I'm the quickest."

"I'd beat all of you," Otis said.

Padovan put his cigarette to his mouth and sucked the hell out of it. Then he exhaled, clouding his space. "I'm the toughest guy here. I would win on toughness."

"You're the strangest guy here," Charlie said. "You would win on being strange."

"Fuck you, Charlie."

Carl disregarded the taunts and looked at me. "How about you, Burt?"

"I'm the quickest guy here. I don't know if I'm the fastest."

Carl opened his meaty hands. "I'll tell you what . . . Twenty bucks to the winner . . . Right now. Once around the block."

Carl paid the bill and we made our way outside, into very cold air. The pavement was still damp from the passing rain, and the street lamp made it glisten. There were no puddles in sight because the rainwater had run off the crowned street into the drains.

We lined up by height. Charlie at 6′4″, took the inside lane, followed by Padovan and Henry at 6′3″, then the 6′2″ Otis Davis, and me at 5′8″. Everyone kept his jacket on except Padovan who wore a white T-shirt . . . but he was from the mean streets of San Pedro.

"Remember," Carl said. "Once around the block. Start here and finish here." He turned to Padovan who took a last puff of his cigarette. "You ready, Padovan?"

"Fuck everybody but me," he responded.

I leaned over and glanced at him. *He's a 100-watt bulb in a 50-watt socket.*

Henry crouched low, and said, "That means he's ready."

Carl yelled at the top of his lungs, "Go!"

And we were off. A little slippery for me the first few steps as my leather soles tried and failed to gain traction. But soon I was leading the pack as we turned the corner, about 75 yards out, hearing everyone else's leather soles pounding the pavement behind me. We sprinted under a lamppost, past a few darkened retail shops on our right. Charlie rallied and closed in on me as we rounded the corner, as he uttered, "Charlie can. Charlie can."

Somewhere behind me, Henry said, "Those cigarettes will kill you Padovan."

On the far side of the block, I was breathing fire, feeling my hamburger coming back up, when I heard someone's shoes closing in fast. It was Otis. Hardly breathing, demonstrating tremendous endurance, he easily passed me. But I didn't give up.

Coming around the last turn my body heated up and I unzipped my wool car coat. By this time, my legs were heavy, filled with lactic acid.

Under the lamppost next to the restaurant, Otis won by a good fifty yards. I stumbled in second, put my hands on my knees and continued to suck air. Henry finished third, followed by Padovan and Charlie.

Carl was waiting at the designated finish mark, and handed Otis his winnings. Charlie, gasping for air, said that Otis cheated because he's got three lungs, whereupon Otis countered, "I'm just better than you."

"Rematch," Charlie said.

"You must like pain," Otis responded, as he slipped the bill in his wallet.

Chapter 9

I sat up front with Otis on the drive back to campus in Carl's four-door, '52 Chevy. The windows fogged as we caught our breath from the run, prompting Carl to crank his down. With cold air now rushing in, Carl said with dripping sincerity, "Burt, how would you like to earn some quick cash?"

In Boyle Heights that question means five-to-ten if you were caught.

"What are you thinking about?" I said with deep suspicion.

"I'd like to start up a dry cleaning business on campus." He paused, like he wanted his words to sink in. "You pick up the clothes and deliver. I'll clean them."

I'm exhausted after working out. But I need the money. "What's my cut?"

"A third of what I make. There's enough business out there for both of us."

We entered campus, slowed to meet the speed limit, and passed dark houses on Fraternity Row, as I thought, *fraternity and sorority members have the money to dry clean, but not the time to run to the 13th Street cleaners a half mile away. I could pick up and deliver on Monday and Wednesday nights right after hashing.*

"Okay, it's a deal."

Carl dropped Henry and me at the Christian House on 13th. Upstairs in Henry's bare-bones room, he put a Sinatra record on his portable turntable and I heard, "No, you can't take that away from me." It was the same record they used to have in the Jazz Room.

I did my best to settle in a beat-up wood chair at his desk and asked him something that had been on my mind for a few days. "How did Padovan get to Oregon?"

Henry flipped through a 78 long-play collection next to his window, apparently deciding what to play next. Without turning back, he said, "He played on a state championship team at Harbor College. That's how Belko heard about him."

"How old is Padovan?"

"Twenty-five. He was in the Navy after he quit high school."

"Quit school?"

"Yeah. He was a tenth grader playing in the L.A. City Basketball Tournament. During the game, the opposing center nailed Padovan's team's big man, knocking him down. Padovan went after the guy and decked him. The crowd booed Padovan and an official threw him out of the game. Then Padovan gave the finger to the crowd, stormed out of the gym, quit school and joined the Navy."

"That explains a lot. Anything else you want to tell me?"

"He's a great friend, but someone you don't want as your enemy."

Chapter 10

On Monday, I met graduate student Mark Elliot in the large gymnastics room for my quickness test. I was eager to find out how I compared with other Oregon athletes. During my last community college baseball season, I was timed in the 50-yard dash at 5.20, in baseball cleats. Later, I learned that my time was one-tenth off the world record.

But I was in the big-time now, where quickness was a given.

The side horse, parallel bars, and high bar had been moved against the far walls for this test. While Elliot checked the electronic connections on his equipment, I stood in the middle of the room in high-top Converse shoes and white shorts, ready to prove myself.

A three-inch high wood take-off box, large enough for me to stand on, was in the center of the room. It was connected by wires to three similar size boxes spread out in three directions, each about twelve feet from the take-off box. One box was straight ahead, one at ten o'clock and one at two o'clock. A bulb and a flat switch were on each of the destination boxes.

Elliot, in khakis and a white T-shirt, explained, "When standing on the take-off box, you sprint forward, left or right, to the box whose bulb has lit up. Shut off the bulb by hitting the flat switch on the top edge of the box."

"Who has the quickest time?" I asked.

Elliot, holding a stopwatch in one hand and a small black box with three switches in the other, said, "Jack Morris, the halfback, is the quickest guy so far. Of course, he's run a 9.6 hundred-yard dash."

Ready to jump out of my skin, I stepped up on the take-off box and waited for a light to go off. Within two seconds, the bulb directly in front of me brightened. I took off with everything I had, reached down, shut it off and slammed into a horsehair-matted wall five yards away.

"Good," said Elliot, as I pried myself off the wall. "Now get back on the platform and get ready for the next light."

I did. Took a deep breath and felt a sharp rib pain. But I said nothing. Guys from East L.A. take pain, don't complain.

"How was my time?"

"Pretty good. Third best so far."

I returned to the box, thinking, *third best isn't good enough.* I bent my knees slightly, and leaned forward, ready to explode off the box. This time the light to my right came on and I shot for it. In no time, I hit the switch, kept going, and my arms pounded into a wrestling mat that was draped over a side-horse, a few yards behind the light.

"Very good," Elliot remarked. "Second best time so far. Now watch for the last light."

I took a deep breath, didn't pay attention to the rib pain. I was going to leave my mark at the university. There was only one light that hadn't gone off, the one to my left. Assuming a slight crouch on the stand, I glanced at the open double doors directly behind the box that led to a hallway. Nothing was going to stop me. I leaned to my left, my muscles charged up. The light to my left lit up. I sprung out, hit the switch quickly, then tried to pull up. But my momentum rocketed me through the open doors and down a short hallway. In an instant, I extended my arms and hit a dead-end wall. To my surprise, my arms ripped through a flimsy wall, then my abdomen hit a horizontal two-by-four, bracing the wall, knocking the wind out of me like a burst balloon. I went limp, collapsed on my back and gasped for air.

Students poured out of the classroom that I had just thrust my arms through. They gathered around me and stared down.

"What happened," asked a male voice.

A coed said, "Two arms shot through the wall on both sides of the professor's head, like Frankenstein got loose."

"Who is he?" Another guy asked.

"Never seen him before."

"Best time ever," an unemotional Mark Elliot said, staring down at me.

Chapter 11

Being the "dry cleaner guy" turned out to be as unprofitable as crashing through the classroom wall. After several weeks of rushing out of the dorm after serving dinner to deliver and pick up garments from the houses, I wasn't making much money and I was burning up energy. I tired quickly during baseball workouts and my timing was off during hitting practice in the field house.

The only benefit in the cleaning business was occasionally wearing expensive sweaters and jackets of my male customers that I held for a few days after they were cleaned. Ever since elementary school, when I wore hand-me-down clothes from my cousin in New York, I swore that my attire would be fashionable. That attitude, however, had some drawbacks.

One night, upon returning from the library, I crossed paths with a guy who called out my name. I stopped and stared at him, but the dimly lit walkway made it difficult to recognize anyone immediately. He wasn't a baseball player, or a basketball player, or from my dorm.

The guy raised his voice. "Burt, I'm Jerry. I gave you my Oregon jacket to be cleaned two weeks ago. When am I going to get it back?"

Shit! I'm wearing his jacket. Beige leather sleeves, green body. His name's on it. Too large for me. Looks like I shrunk inside it.

"I'm picking it up tomorrow," I said, hoping he would be into that.

"Hey, that looks like my jacket your wearing."

"Oh, no. This one's not yours."

"My name is on it."

Think of something.

"This is Jerry Shipley's jacket," I said without a hint of panic. "He loaned it to me. Don't worry; yours had some spots that had to be removed. They had to wait for the spot remover to dry."

"Two weeks for the spot remover to dry? Just give it back."

Get out of this business. It's too stressful and energy depleting. Only perk is wearing nice clothes.

"I'll get it for you tomorrow." I turned and walked away into the darkness of my life.

Chapter 12

I had retired from the dry cleaning business by the time the Cal basketball team came to town on a Saturday night in early February. Henry knew Joe Kapp, the Cal quarterback who was also the Bears second-string center. The 6′4″ Kapp roomed with a high school (Roosevelt, L.A.) friend of ours, Ned Averbuck, who was now starring on the Cal freshman basketball team. Cal was leading the conference, one game ahead of Oregon State. But I didn't have conference standings on my mind when I approached Charlie and presented an idea in a busy locker room an hour before game time. I was thinking about having enough money to eat on Sunday when the cafeteria was closed.

"Charlie," I said. "You're not using your game tickets. How about letting me sell them? I'll give you half of what they go for. It's a good deal for both of us."

Charlie gave me a hard look. "That would be okay, but it's got to pay." He handed me his tickets.

"I'll pay you right after the game," I said, confident I could sell his tickets, and ready to go outside and battle the rain in my heavy tweed overcoat.

"Be sure you do, or you'll deal with you know who."

I gave him thumbs up, turned toward Henry, a couple of lockers away, to make a ticket deal with him. But he was in the middle of what was on its way to be a heated conversation with a player who used the next locker. While unbuttoning his vertically striped oxford shirt, Henry said that he hoped his friend Joe Kapp would play well.

"How can you say that?" the player shot back. "We're playing against him."

Henry raised his voice slightly. "He's my friend, and I pull for my friends."

"But we're playing against him. That's not right."

"It is right," Henry growled. "I still want to win, but I want him to play well."

"But if he plays well, we might lose."

Henry unraveled. "I'm going to say this one more fuckin' time! I hope he plays well and we win!"

At that moment, my intuition told me to get the hell out of there before Henry decked another guy. It was time to test the marketplace.

It was still raining when I walked to the dimly lit corner above the baseball stadium, a half-block from the arena, to sell Charlie's tickets. Although I had never sold tickets before, I had watched ticket scalpers operate in front of L.A.'s Coliseum before football games when I was a peanut vendor in the eighth and ninth grades. So I was optimistic when plenty of fans were coming my way. Four tickets for seven bucks each, face value, was going to be a snap.

With rainwater streaming down my face, I yelled, "Tickets, tickets right here!" Fans passed me like I had leprosy. I pulled up the collar of my overcoat, stopping the trickle down my neck, and barked, "Hey, Charlie Franklin's tickets right here."

Two more guys passed by. *Something's wrong. Maybe they won't buy a Black guy's tickets?*

I came back with, "Great seats. Great seats right here!" A tall middle-aged man wearing a beige raincoat, a dripping black umbrella over his head, stopped. So did a few adults behind him.

"Whatya got?" the man asked suspiciously.

I gave him a sincere look. I had no idea where the seats were, but I was anxious to unload them. "Four great seats at cost."

After the transaction, I kept my distance from the buyer, watching him when I crossed over to the other side of the street, fearful that he would learn at the ticket window that the seats were not so great. I stood under a tree across from the Mac Court entrance when the buyer entered the arena. Then I entered the arena.

In Navy blue and gold warm-ups, Cal was the antithesis of Oregon during the pre-game period. It was like the circus was in town. They displayed great spirit, talking it up during a basic lay-up drill, like they owned the place. Oregon, on the other hand, quietly went about their business of getting warmed up for the game with common three-man drills.

Once again, Otis impressed me with his elevation during lay-ups, getting his eyes on the ten-foot rim before dropping in the ball. He was no ordinary athlete. And I thought he could also make his mark as a high jumper.

Sitting shoulder-to-shoulder in the cheering section with a bunch of students who didn't understand basketball very well, I watched Otis bring the ball down during the early stage of the game, with one eye on a screaming Belko, and one eye on his defender—a tall order for a mere mortal. It was apparent that Belko didn't trust him. Nor did Belko trust Henry and Padovan that week. In fact, trust appeared to be moment-to-moment with Belko.

The game turned out to be a nightmare for the Ducks. They couldn't defend against Cal's fluid offense, while Cal prevented the ball from going in to Charlie, holding him to ten points.

Henry played well, consistently hitting the open man with accurate passes. But Belko limited his playing time—perhaps teaching Henry a lesson for cold-cocking his teammate. And Padovan was still in Belko's doghouse for not giving up smoking.

After the game, most of the players had left the locker room by the time I entered to pay off Charlie. Only Henry, Padovan, and Charlie remained. I paid off Charlie, who nodded and said, "Right, 'Ol Fade." Then I waited for Henry to tie his shoes so we could get going.

Standing near the adjoining equipment room, I watched Padovan hand in his uniform to the basketball manager, who received it above a half Dutch door. Then, Padovan froze in place when he spotted a black Iowa warm-up jacket with gold and white lettering that hung from a clothesline behind the manager.

"Hey!" Padovan said, pointing to the warm-up, "That's mine."

"No, George. That's on display," the manager said, his head sinking into this neck. "A company that makes uniforms gave it to us as an example of their work."

"That warm-up is mine," repeated Padovan, with madness in his voice.

"You don't understand," the manager said, as if Padovan was an idiot. "That belongs to the athletic department."

There was fire in Padovan's eyes now, and he roared, "No, you don't understand. That's mine! Give it to me or I'll kill you!"

The manager considered his options for moment, then reached back and handed over the warm-up, whereupon Padovan put it on and exited he room.

And I stood there thinking, *he's the same guy who gave the finger to the crowd, then walked out of the gym and joined the Navy. Anything is possible with him.*

*   *   *

The Cal Bears had finished eating their post-game meal in the student union by the time Henry, Padovan, and I arrived to see Joe Kapp. Up close, the 6'4" Kapp was short for a center, but the long scar on his cheek indicated that he wasn't the kind of guy who would back down from anything. In other words, I guessed he was in the mold of Padovan and Henry. Kapp had no trouble directing us, saying that he liked to walk each campus the Bears visited. He glanced at Padovan's Iowa jacket, but said nothing and started to walk out of the union with us tagging along. The four of us were comfortably dressed for the brisk temperature, Henry in an Oregon letterman's jacket, Kapp in a beige raincoat over a blue blazer, and me in my all-purpose gray wool overcoat.

The rain had stopped and the crowned streets had shed water toward the gutter and were almost dry. We followed Kapp down 13th Street talking basketball. Kapp said, "I think you guys are a better team than you showed us tonight."

"I know we are," Henry responded, doing his best to keep up with Kapp who led us like he was a parade.

"We played big tonight," Kapp said.

Padovan said sharply, "We'll be ready by the time we play you in Berkeley."

A couple of blocks into our journey, Kapp turned into a dark alley. I was reluctant to follow, but did. My experience had been that in East Los Angeles you never walked into a dark alley unless you wanted to put your life on the line. But Kapp chuckled and said the last alley he walked into was in Manhattan after Cal played in Madison Square Garden. "That's when a guy tried to mug me and I beat the shit out of him. But he slashed my face."

* * *

It was difficult to see anything in the alley. Low clouds had covered the moon. Halfway down a long stretch, still talking basketball, someone nearby shouted, "Fuck Cal."

Bizarre! A disgruntled fan waiting in a dark alley for us?

"Who said that?" Kapp barked, surveying the darkness, finally focusing on what appeared to be a parked car about fifteen feet away, parallel to the fence.

"Over here, asshole!" a man called out.

We approached the car slowly. The driver's side window was down and there was a dark figure behind the wheel. Kapp, now within reach of the car, cocked his fist as if he was going to throw a punch, but he was met with the thrust of Padovan's forearm against his chest. Kapp slapped Padovan's arm down. "He's mine, George."

"No, Joe, he's mine," countered Padovan, pushing Kapp away.

Kapp roared, "No, he's mine!"

Kapp and Padovan squared off, ready to fight each other over who was going to throw the first punch at the man. Then Kapp refocused, stepped forward and took a wild swing through an open window, hitting the man's chest. "Oh, shit," Kapp said, pulling away from the window frame, shaking his hand vigorously. "The guy's got a body cast on."

The man said nothing.

We walked away in silence, like nothing had happened—as if we were at an amusement park, failed to win a prize at a booth, and just moved on. But I couldn't help thinking, *I am with human volcanoes. What's next?*

Chapter 13

By mid-February, I had enticed seven players to let me sell their tickets, including three players from the state of Oregon, despite weekly negative articles in the campus newspaper about California and Californians. That was something, to have the Oregon guys trust a Californian.

Ticket sales were netting me $49 per game, almost as much as I made hashing each month. With a couple of home games left, it appeared as though I would earn enough to fill my gas tank until Spring break and eat every Sunday.

But something had to give. Although I was no longer in the cleaning business, my horrendous schedule was sucking every bit of energy out of me athletically and academically. A week after the Cal game, I was trudging from my dorm to the field house in a light shower, when I felt the symptoms of a bad cold coming on. And something else was bothering me. I headed for the infirmary.

I found the one-story brick building oddly placed across campus where it was a struggle for any sick student to get there. Uncomfortable as hell, I waited for service, having a hard time understanding why the patient always waits for the doctor.

Finally, I was ushered into an austere office with bare walls and a couple of instruments strewn on a desk. The young doctor took my temperature. I assumed he was the doctor. He was wearing a white lab coat, a means of identity for all doctors.

After I answered a few basic questions, he said, "Get lots of rest, drink plenty of water. You'll be fine in a couple of days."

"But what about my skin?" I asked.

He took a moment to study me like I was a museum piece. "What do you mean?"

"My skin. It's white. When I came up a few months ago my skin was tan. I'm sick."

"Yes. You're Caucasian."

"No. There's something wrong with me."

The doctor read my chart and looked up with an ear-to-ear grin. "Says here you're from Los Angeles. You just haven't seen any sun for a while. That's all."

I thought about my life in L.A. A lot of time playing baseball under a hot sun. My skin had been tan forever. No wonder.

The doctor added, "You're a hypochondriac."

"Well," I said. "Even hypochondriacs get sick."

* * *

On Sunday, Henry invited Padovan and me to the Christian House for lunch. The bottom floor was large and dark, with mahogany walls and floors. Several distressed picnic tables were lined up end-to-end, with twenty chairs. Henry had warned us that there was a nickel fine for every table manner mistake. I didn't know table manners, but through observation I quickly learned that I could be penalized by talking to the wrong person, passing food incorrectly, or using the wrong utensil.

Henry took a seat next to me and Padovan sat directly across from Henry. Then Padovan yelled to a guy at the end of the table. "Hey, you, pass the bread," instead of politely saying, "please pass the bread," to the guy sitting next to him. Although that was a nickel fine, Padovan wasn't charged. When the bread dish was passed his way, Padovan's long fingers snatched seven slices when he was only supposed to take one.

But again nothing was said. Instead members sitting next to him shook their heads.

Chuck Mitchelmore, the editor of the *Daily Emerald*, the university newspaper, tried to trick me into engaging in conversations with him. Mitchelmore, who was very proper, appeared older than he was. He sat at one end of the table, and I was three chairs to his left. He asked, "Burt, how do you like your hamburger?" I did not respond. Communication at the table, I learned quickly, was only permitted with people sitting next to you, in front of you, or diagonally across from you. I had to laugh when that move cost Mitchelmore a nickel. So did he. Padovan, on the other hand, gave me a quizzical look and grabbed some more bread.

As Padovan stuffed his mouth with hamburger, he told Henry about his friend Germ, a former community college teammate from San Pedro. He said Germ was 27 years-old and had played for seven colleges around the country in seven years. "Every year," Padovan said, "Germ uses the same community college transcript and gets a basketball scholarship at another college in a different part of the country. Then he plays, doesn't attend class, and flunks out at the end of the season."

My take: *Germ was clearly Padovan's hero. Someone who could get away with something. But strange.*

Standing on the front porch after lunch, Padovan said to me, "Hey, you hash at the dorm. How about getting my family some food? We're starving up here."

I was surprised to learn during lunch that Padovan was married and had a newborn baby boy. And I felt terrible that the athletic department wasn't taking care of his family's basic needs. But what could I do? I couldn't get him meals.

"I don't get it, George. What are you saying?"

"Eggs . . . get us some eggs, man."

My take: *There's a problem. You're my friend. Solve it.*

Chapter 14

The following week, while serving students in the hash line, my supervisor told me to take the elevator down to the food storage area and retrieve large containers of ice cream from the freezer.

After a rickety ride down, I found the large freezer, a sub-zero walk-in that froze my breath in mid-air. I secured two large tubs of ice cream, then quickly surveyed the rest of the storeroom. Super large cans and large boxes of food. Strawberries, potato chips, and in the cooler, cartons of eggs that I needed for Padovan. *Food service*, I thought, *would never miss a dozen eggs here or there, and Padovan won't have to starve.*

I placed the ice cream on the floor, stood on a wood crate, and unsnapped a window which was at ground level of the alley.

Two nights later at 3 a.m., my heart pounding away, I entered the dark alley adjacent to the to the food storage room, opened the window and slid my legs through. When I was halfway in, a screen hook latched onto my jacket, causing the screen to rattle. I held my breath and listened to the sound of silence. Then I wedged my body through, after releasing the hook. Inside, assisted by a smidgen of light from the alley, I planted my feet on the crate I had set up earlier. I quickly found the eggs, placed six dozen in a small box, and slid them out the window into the alley. After crawling out, I shut the window, fixed the screen, and stored the eggs in the trunk of my car, hoping that a 40-degree temperature wouldn't spoil them.

Then next morning when a rising sun brightened the campus, I arrived at Padovan's ground floor apartment. I knocked on the door. In seconds, Padovan opened it. Standing in his skivvies with a blank face, he said, "Burt, what are you doing here?"

"I filled your order. You needed eggs, I got eggs. Six dozen of them."

He gave me a confused look. "What order?"

"Eggs. I got you the eggs." I extended my arms. "Here, take 'em."

Padovan's mouth dropped, his thick eyebrows drew together.

"Look, I have to go to breakfast. Enjoy."

Stumbling for words, he said, "Ah, hey, how 'bout you and Henry having breakfast with us? I'll call him. Come in."

I entered his small apartment feeling awkward. Padovan, who claimed that his family was starving, was going to share their food with us. But I went along with it. While waiting for Henry, my butt on a hardwood chair in a tiny front room, I read an article in *Sports Illustrated* about an amazing basketball player at the University of Seattle named Elgin Baylor. Looking around the room, I wondered where we were going to eat and what we were going to eat. There was a small sofa, a lamp table, and a twelve-inch black and white TV with rabbit ears positioned on a short stack of bricks, across the room.

Minutes later, Henry, who had borrowed a car, showed up.

My attention turned to the kitchen a few feet away where Padovan broke egg after egg in a large fry pan, nonstop. It turned out to be the largest scrambled egg order I had ever seen. *I'm pissed. I stole all those eggs for one meal. Either his family wasn't starving or he's a nut case.*

"What the hell are you doing, George?" I asked.

"Haven't you ever seen six dozen scrambled eggs before?" Padovan asked with a wicked smile. "I was a cook in the Navy. Used to cook for several hundred people. I don't know how to cook for a few people."

"That's 18 eggs for each of us," his petite blonde wife who suddenly appeared, said. She snuggled up to Padovan in the tight kitchen, as he whisked another batch of eggs.

"I don't count," Padovan said. "I just cook."

Finally, Henry and I sat on the floor and Padovan and his wife occupied the sofa, as we all ate "endless eggs." The eggs were good, but too much of a good thing. And Padovan was happy.

Someone cared about him and he got to relive his Navy days. And I fell for a bad joke and didn't like it very much.

*   *   *

As Padovan washed dishes, he spoke to Henry, who stood a few feet from him in the living room. "I'll meet you in the locker room."

"What's up?" I asked.

"Oregon State," Henry said. "We're going to play in the big house—Gill Coliseum seats 12,000. The largest arena we'll play in this year."

"Sounds exciting."

I followed Henry back to the Christian House. There, he returned the car he had borrowed and I drove toward Mac Court, passing the red-brick law school on 13th. Henry said, "I told you Padovan was an interesting guy."

I volumed up. "I was stupid stealing those eggs. I could have gone to jail like Jean Valjean in *Les Miserables* . . . That's the last favor I'm doing for him."

Henry laughed. "I can't believe you took him seriously."

"Don't talk to me."

As I turned right and approached Mac Court, Henry said, "I need to turn in a paper to Sigerseth, but I don't have time. I left it in my locker. Would you mind turning it in for me?"

"After I pay everyone for their tickets. But I'm not getting you any eggs."

Downstairs, the locker room was packed with players, including Padovan, who hurriedly prepared to get on the bus to Oregon State, an hour away. Small Kelly-green travel bags with the words Oregon Basketball on the side were being handed out by the manager, who stood on the other side of the Dutch door in the equipment room. I waited by the doorway with a roll of bills in one hand, watching the players check the bag's contents: one green uniform; one warm-up jersey; one jock; two pairs of white wool socks; one pair of white, high-top Converse basketball shoes.

As players began to exit, I handed my business partners their take of the last game. While this was going on, Hal Duffy—the 6′ 5″, 240-pound, cherub-faced center—got the canvas ball bag from the manager. Holding the bag in one hand and his travel bag in the other, he approached Padovan, who was checking his gear.

"Here, rookie," Duffy said. "Carry the balls."

Padovan gave Duffy a hard look and punched him in the mouth, staggering Duffy.

"Oh, shit!" the manager said, who took off upstairs, probably to report Padovan, who he still hated for taking the Iowa warm-up.

"You son of a bitch," Duffy barked, slamming a much lighter Padovan against the lockers. "Why did you do that?"

"I'm no fuckin' rookie," Padovan yelled, as he pushed Duffy back. "I'm 25 years old. I've been in the Navy. And I'm from S.P., Jack."

Duffy stared at Padovan. Evidently he didn't get it.

I got it. Never confront someone from S.P.

I could hear the manager rambling in the hallway, outside the locker room. "Padovan hit Duffy for no reason. Padovan hit Duffy for no reason."

Coach Belko stormed into the room, appraised Duffy, who had blood trickling from the corner of his mouth, then turned to Padovan. "What happened?"

"Ask Duffy."

"Nothing," Duffy said. "Nothing happened."

Belko said sharply, "You guys need to take your aggression out on Oregon State. Now get on the bus." Then he looked at me. "I told you to stay out. You've got no business here."

"Yes, Sir," I said. But thought, *I do have a going business here.*

Chapter 15

In the boxing gym that afternoon I was taking out my aggressions on the heavy bag and feeling relieved. Two guys in my weight class were absent and I wouldn't have to fight anyone that day. Although I could be aggressive, I wasn't an angry person, and I disliked hitting someone for no reason. Case in point, one of my partners was a track guy from Australia, a very poor fighter. When I had to face him, I would land a couple of punches that he couldn't handle, then feel sorry for him and limit contact.

All of a sudden, the coach's voice echoed in the gym when he said, "Burt, it's time for you to get in the ring. Where's your partner?"

"All the guys in my weight are absent, Coach," I said. "I don't fight today."

"Oh, yes you do. You have to fight every day. Now who are you going to fight?"

He's insane. "There's no one here in my weight class."

"Doesn't matter. You have to fight someone."

That's when I gave him an East L.A. false bravado response. "I don't care. Put anyone in there." As soon as I said that I wanted to take back those words. But I knew I had cooked myself. That was all the blood-thirsty coach had to hear.

All movement and conversations in the gym suddenly stopped. All eyes were on the coach. I could feel the tension in the room.

"Heard," the coach growled. "Bob Heard. Get in there."

Shit. Mr. Mean. My death warrant. Two hundred sixty pounds of kick-ass trouble. A defensive lineman who lived to maim the quarterback.

Heard climbed into the ring and sneered at me like he wanted to break my face. Then he pounded his chest and roared. I slipped between the ropes trying to show no fear while my heart did a drum roll. I went to my corner, straightened my headgear and hoped for a miracle. But the bell rang anyway. We touched gloves in the center of the ring. That was as friendly as Heard got. From there, I kept my distance, circling him from right to left, my head bobbing and weaving, hoping to bore the hell out of him.

Someone's voice came through the tiny ear hole in my headgear. "Protect yourself, Burt."

Heard stalked me like a starving lion and I kept dancing away, thinking, *ring the goddamn bell. Ring the bell.*

After about two minutes of evasive tactics, I wound up in a corner, trapped. Heard threw a left hook like he was swinging a two-by-four. I saw it coming all the way. My right glove-hand protecting the right side of my headgear blocked his punch. But it felt like I rammed a brick wall. My lights went out, and I fell into a dark abyss that had no bottom.

Sometime afterward, I opened my eyes with my nose flat on the mat, wondering why I was there.

"He's breathing," a voice said.

I struggled to my knees, remembering that I had blocked Heard's punch. I stood, my legs wobbly, my head fuzzy, and slowly exited the ring. It was one of the most valuable lessons I learned at Oregon: Think twice before you open your big fuckin' mouth.

Chapter 16

It was the last weekend in February, the last two basketball games of the season. Oregon was in the Bay Area to play conference-leader Cal on Friday night, followed the next night with a game at Stanford. The first night, I listened to the Cal game on the dorm's floor model radio, alone, half studying in the lounge, then pacing back and forth when the announcer said repeatedly, "Basket by Padovan," and "Basket by Ronquillo." When Oregon led by four late in the second half, a loud roar went up from the crowd as if something spectacular had happened. The announcer shouted, "Oh, my God. There's a cadaver's arm on the floor in Cal's offensive court. The arm was just tossed out of the men's cheering section and caromed off Ronquillo's leg. Now that section is yelling in unison, 'Call the foul.'"

When sanity was restored several minutes later, the announcer reported that Henry and Padovan continued to hit their shots. At game's end, Oregon upset Cal by ten, hitting 65 percent of their field goals, and I felt good that my friends had done so well.

Saturday night, I settled back in the dorm lounge again and listened to Stanford beat Oregon easily. This time, Henry and Padovan did not play, which I didn't understand since they had performed so well the previous night.

Late in the morning the next day, there was a knock at my door.

Henry swung it open, ducked under the doorframe, and stopped. His eyes could have bored a hole in the linoleum floor. His square shoulders were slumped. His face was ashen. The team was supposed to return to Eugene by train in the late afternoon. But there he was.

"What happened?" I asked.

Answers rolled off Henry's tongue as if hot lights were on him at the precinct.

"Belko put Padovan and me on a train yesterday," he said softly. "We missed the Stanford game."

"But you guys were the stars of the Cal game."

"We got in trouble after the game. The first part was good. In that crazy gym we tore Cal up. Everything we shot went in. We were all-time happy after the game. Then Kapp invited us to his apartment for a party. And we decided to celebrate."

"Joe Kapp, the Cal quarterback?"

"Yeah."

"So how'd you guys get in trouble?"

Henry shook his head. "We didn't get back to the hotel until three. Belko was waiting for us in the lobby. The manager told Belko we weren't in our rooms at bed check. And you know how the manager hates Padovan. Remember, Padovan told the manager he was going to kill him before he stole the Iowa warm-up."

"He's still mad about that?"

Henry went on, "Belko suspended us. Now we're off the team until he makes a decision to keep us or cut us sometime this Spring. But we still have our scholarship until then."

I shook my head. "Horrible, man."

Henry crossed the room, sank into Aki's chair. "It was great party. All the Cal players were there. And the place was crawling with chicks. Kapp told me to pick out a girl for the evening. I looked around and spotted this gorgeous blonde on the other side of the living room with a drink in her hand, talking to one of the Cal players. I pointed at her. 'How about the blonde?'

"Kapp put his arm on my shoulder and yelled across the room, 'Hey,

Laura. This is Henry. You're going to be with him tonight.'

"I found out later that was Kapp's girl."

Kapp IS a different guy.

Henry pushed off the chair like an old man. Slowly and methodically. "Let's go over to Padovan's and see how he's doing."

We headed for my car across the street. The sun was unusually warm, maybe in the fifties, and for the first time in Eugene I wore a short sleeve shirt. I noticed that Henry, who normally walked with his shoulders upright, his chest out, and his arms swinging slightly behind his back, now was hunched over, his strut a shuffle.

As we got into my car I thought, *how is he going to explain his situation to his parents? Very proud people. Proud of his brother, Manuel, captain of the USC track team, who graduated with honors.*

I started up my car. The brown naugahyde seats were warm and stretched. The needle on the gas gauge was a hair above empty. Henry and I treated the car like a juke box, only putting in a quarter for a gallon every time we took her out. We hadn't run out yet, but we were close.

I drove toward Padovan's apartment, past blocks of old, gray wood-slat houses. Stop signs were nowhere, potholes everywhere. I glanced at Henry. *His spirit's gone.*

He usually enjoyed life's simple pleasures, or created them if they were not coming his way. In high school he was known for being the guy who brought a jug of wine and shared it in the bathroom during lunchtime. It was never cigarettes, marijuana, or bennies. I remembered tasting the wine. God-awful.

* * *

In Padovan's living room, cardboard boxes were strewn everywhere. Padovan, wearing the Iowa warm-up, was packing his clothes in a large carton. His wife, once again in curlers, said nothing while clanging a few pots and pans into a small box.

"I'm getting the fuck out of here!" snapped Padovan while redistributing pots.

"Hang in there, man," Henry said. "Belko will let you back on the team."

"Fuck this place and everyone in it."

I stood over him. *He's pissing away a scholarship, something I desperately wanted.*

"Be patient," Henry said. "It's only your life you're talking about."

"Fuck it!" Padovan reacted. "The Medak Basketball Tournament starts tomorrow in San Pedro. I'll be there. I'll be on Germ's team."

The yellow phone on the kitchen wall rang. Padovan worked his way through a maze of cardboard boxes and picked it up. "Yeah." He listened, then smiled at Henry. "It's Germ."

Germ, who went to seven colleges in seven years. Germ, whose only goal is to play basketball.

Standing in the middle of the clutter, Henry pleaded with Padovan. "Don't give up your education, man."

"What time's the first game?" Padovan asked Germ. He nodded. "I'll be there. S.P. will clean house on those cats." He hung up. "The first game's at seven tomorrow night. If I leave now, I'll make it. It's only a fourteen-hour drive down the 99."

"What should I tell Belko?" Henry asked.

"Tell him the Iowa warm-up is walking around S.P." He reached behind a box in the living room, picked up his travel bag, and handed it to Henry. "Hand in this piece of shit uniform for me."

We shook hands with Padovan and told him how much we'd miss him. Back in the car, Henry placed Padovan's bag in the backseat and then turned to me. "He's making a big mistake. It's his last chance to get an education."

As we rolled toward campus, there was silence for a long moment as if we were memorializing Padovan. Then I said, "If he doesn't have basketball, he has nothing. He's probably going back to the docks." I pressed down on the gas pedal and veered left, avoiding a few potholes. "Maybe he'll be happier as a longshoreman."

"If he lives that long."

Chapter 17

The baseball team worked out in the football field house during the winter months while waiting for the sun to come out. Playing baseball within those confines was depressing and claustrophobic. I had already lived through elementary school days with asthma, in bed half the year, gasping for air. Although I grew out of the asthma by age nine, the uneasy feeling of being inside was still with me.

That's what I was thinking while circling the arena at top speed with the rest of the team. It was several days after Padovan had evacuated the city and the tail end of my winter of discontent. During my run, I watched my shoes hit the unvarnished floor on the outside portion of the sole, something I had become conscious of during my high school playing days. But as hard as I tried, I couldn't land the ball of my foot flat on the hardwood. As I pursued correctness, I thought: *An adjustment means greater push-off power. I'd be in Mickey Mantle's league. He was 3.1 to first base as a lefty. I could challenge that time.*

My mind in another universe, I watched a pack of runners in dark green sweats thunder past me. Trailing them around a turn, I noticed a tall, bald man near the arena entrance who held a stopwatch in one hand while barking at the runners, "Swing your arms freely from your shoulders." *This guy knows running fundamentals. Maybe he could help me.*

After I completed my laps, I stopped where this man was coaching.

Drenched in sweat, catching my breath, I waited for him to finish talking to ten athletes who were gathered around him. As I approached him, he started to jog away. I didn't know if he was avoiding me, or if that was his normal gait. Doing my best to keep up with him after a tiring workout, I asked, "Are you the track coach?"

He didn't turn to look at me, kept jogging. "They call me Coach Bowerman," he said, like I needed to show him a little more respect.

"Coach Bowerman, I wonder if you can help me. I'm on the baseball team. When I sprint, I land on the outside of my shoes. I know I would be quicker if I hit on the balls of my feet. How can I do that?"

We entered the hallway of the P.E. building, avoided oncoming students and moving past office door after office door. Finally, he answered. "Try walking pigeon-toed. Eventually you'll hit squarely on the ball of your foot."

"Thanks. How long will it take to do that?"

"About a year," he said, turning a corner. And like smoke, he was gone in a second.

After receiving that important bit of advice, I walked all day, every day, with my toes pointed in. Every time I approached a glass entrance door, I looked at my reflection to see how I was doing. After a while, I noticed that several basketball players also walked pigeon-toed. And I wondered if Bowerman had reached them, or if they were born that way.

*　*　*

When the weather became reliably dry, Coach Kirsch moved our workout outdoors. The first day it was like coming out of a dark movie house to bright sunlight. Everything was brighter. Sky. Grass. Everything. And I was so glad to get out of that damn claustrophobic field house. Our two-hour workout was held in the baseball stadium, next to Mac Court, a picturesque setting with bright green grass, cement bleachers down both foul lines that held about 3,000 fans, and an outfield backdrop of deep-green fir trees on the hills a few miles away.

I held my own in batting practice, hitting shots beyond the outfielders. And in offensive and defensive situations I excelled with my quickness, despite still running on the outer edge of my cleats. When we scrimmaged, however, I was not hitting the way I expected and couldn't figure out why. And I usually excelled under pressure. But failing to make the team and not getting a scholarship was always on my mind. So were the words that the doctor told me when I was sixteen, after my dad and I had our car demolished by a ten-ton cement truck. "It's not advisable for you to play baseball anymore," the doctor said. "The wrong kind of contact and you're paralyzed. A diving catch, breaking up a double play, crashing into the catcher to score—that's out. You've cracked a spinal transverse process."

Not words I could live by.

I didn't discuss my personal drama with anyone, certainly not Kirsch who wouldn't permit me to play, or any players who made me feel that they'd just as soon see me go to hell as make the team.

One day, the grass had been mowed just before we took the field. When I took the field my nose ran, my eyes watered, and I sneezed repeatedly. Needing to stave off a cold or worse, my great fear, a return to the symptoms of asthma. I headed for the infirmary after practice. There, the same white-coated doctor who had seen me earlier, asked me, "What's up with you today?"

"Oh, you remember me. I was here because my skin had turned white."

The doctor shook his head, opened my folder. "How could I forget?"

I blew my nose into a damp handkerchief that carried the day's germs. "I'm playing baseball for the university. They cut the grass today and I got cold symptoms standing in the outfield. Now I have a bad cold. I had asthma as a child and don't want to go back there. You see, asthma caused me to be bedridden half the year when I was in elementary school. I'm not going there, am I?"

The doc gave me a long look. The kind of look he gave me the last time I was there. "What position do you play?"

"Center field. What are you getting at?"

"Which way does the wind blow at the ballpark?"

"It blows out, toward center field, my position. Why?"

He noted something in my folder and looked up. "Well, you've got a problem. Can you play another position?"

My heart pumped stronger in reaction to the question. "Why?"

"Because you're allergic to your position. I can give you an allergy shot for grass, but you won't be sensitized until June. By that time your season will be over."

His words dug deep into my soul. "I can't play the infield. I'm left-handed. The only position I could play is first base, but I'm not tall enough. And I can't pitch."

"I'm sorry," the doctor said, closing my folder. "That's the best I can do."

My mind spun. "You're telling me I'm allergic to the game I love."

"Yes. And it's evident you have baseball fever, for which there is no cure."

Chapter 18

S itting deep in a large stuffed chair in the Jazz Room that night, I thought: *This place is supposed to bring peace, relaxation and an ability to concentrate not available anywhere else on campus.* For me, however, it was a place where I was always the recipient of odd ideas.

I glanced at Henry, sitting close by, heavily dressed in preparation of the cold front that was moving through Eugene. There was an unopened textbook on his lap. With Sinatra singing in the background, he turned me. "I need a favor. I—"

Suspicious of those words, I cut him off with, "I'm not taking records or eggs."

Henry glanced at a guy, who sat quietly in the corner, about five yards from us, then put a finger across his lips, and spoke softly. "I need you to take a final for me in Advanced Ed Psych."

"Why can't you take it?"

"I signed up for two classes that are held at the same time. Now the finals are at the same time."

"How did you attend two classes at the same time"?

"I never attended the Ed Psych class. But I know roll was never taken."

"Only one professor teaches the course," I said. "That's Anderson. I have him for another Education class. He'd recognize me. And I can't afford to take that chance. If I got caught, I would never get a scholarship."

"It's a sure thing, man. I have the test. And Anderson never looks at his students. He's always gazing out the window at the chicks. Walk in. Keep your head down. You'll be okay."

"Where'd you get the test?"

Henry said with confidence, "The House saves them. And Anderson has given the same test for three years." He waved a hand. "If I don't pass this class I can't student-teach this Spring. You gotta help me out."

I mulled over his thinking. "You're already on probation. If this blew up, Belko would cancel you. And you're talking to a guy who had his scholarship dropped, stole eggs for no reason, failed in the dry cleaning business, and got knocked out in class. I'm not exactly a winner."

Henry waited a beat, then said, "You took Ernie's finals."

See what shit comes back to bite you in the ass.

I remembered the time and place. East Los Angeles Junior College, one year ago. Two weeks before finals. My long-time friend, Ernie Rodriguez, and I were walking across campus to get lunch, when he said, "I'm leaving to play baseball in Canada tomorrow and I need you to take two finals for me."

I stopped in my tracks, thought he had flipped out. His idea was beyond being baseball crazy. But here was my best friend who I had grown up with, played on the same baseball teams with, and who managed to get me elected high school student body president by splitting the Japanese-American vote. It wasn't that he couldn't pass his finals if he were here. Now he's leaving????

Yeah, Ernie and I went back a long way. When we were kids, we would do anything to become better baseball players. When we were eleven years old, his mother told us that she had heard there was a Cleveland Indian scout who worked with young baseball players at Manchester Playground. "You guys should go there," she said, like it was going down the street. And she gave us directions. The challenge, however, was that we would have to make three trolley transfers to wind up 30 miles from Boyle Heights at Manchester Playground and find the scout Evo Pusich. On several occasions, I had already taken a trolley downtown, a ten-mile ride, to go to a movie by myself. I thought if I could go ten miles, why not thirty.

But Ernie and I got lost in downtown L.A. at the Grand Central Market and had to ask adults behind the fish and produce counters where in the hell we were. Finally, after many hours of travel on rickety trolleys with hard wood seats, our brown bag lunches in one hand and our gloves in the other, we managed to find Manchester Playground, a huge complex of four dirt diamonds. There were a few kids fielding balls hit by adults on each diamond, so we made the long walk to ask the adults on three diamonds, "Are you Evo Pusich?"

At long last, on the fourth field, we found a middle-aged guy working out kids our age on a far diamond. And he showed us how to hold our bats correctly.

I smiled at the thought of that adventure.

* * *

Henry brought me back with, "If you get in trouble, I'll do something to get you out of trouble."

"Like put a Band-Aid on a dead man!"

He's a good friend. I'm experienced. He has the test. I'd be in and out.

* * *

A couple of days later, praying for anonymity, I walked into the large classroom with a flock of students for the Advanced Ed. Psych final. I took a deep breath. There was nothing riding on this, only two scholarships and my baseball career. My head down, I found an open chair in the middle of the room. Soon the place was packed with maybe 200 students and I could feel the tension in the air that came with taking a final. As for me, I was apprehensive and confident, like an expert defusing a bomb.

My eyes jogged left and right. No one looked my way, just the way I liked it. Suddenly, the guy sitting to my left asked me, "Did you study hard?"

Damn it. Mind your own business?

My eyes on my desk, I nodded.

But the guy went on with, "How about the theory of mediocrity?"

"Excuse me. I need to do some last minute studying." I opened the text that Henry gave me. The spine cracked.

About a minute later, Dr. Anderson entered, in preppy attire, with the air of someone who never lost a scrabble game. He gave us a welcoming, "Take everything off your desk except your number two pencil. This should be an easy test. I passed it."

Silence in the room.

Down the aisle came a female teaching assistant passing out tests. I wasn't looking at her when she placed a test on my desk. I signed Henry's name and did my best to slip out a 3″ x 3″ note card from my wool jacket pocket without being noticed. 100 answers printed microscopically with a very sharp pencil point, now cupped in my hand.

My palm down, resting on the desk, I thought, *how many questions should I miss? Ten? Fifteen? How smart do I want to make Henry? Seventeen? Is Henry smart enough to score 83? Yeah. Spread the missed answers around.*

It didn't take long to fill out Henry's answers. I slipped the answer card in my jacket and looked at the clock high on the wall, over the door. I had plenty of time to look like I was still taking the test. I acted like I hadn't finished by moving a finger from question to question, all the while thinking, *can't be first to hand this in. Wait for the right moment. What if Anderson stops me? Dive through the open window next to his desk. Then run like hell ... Why cheat for Henry and not for yourself? Because you are not a cheater, that's why.*

After 40 minutes, a few students walked up the long aisle to hand in their work. A few minutes later, there was a logjam at Anderson's desk. But he was distracted with a passing coed on the walking path. I slipped in Henry's test, scurried to the door. Outside, I ran down the brick steps toward the cemetery, thinking, *this is the end of my stupidity.*

Chapter 19

Two days after winter finals, I searched for my grade in Sigerseth's class by scanning for my name on the typewritten list behind the glass-enclosed case outside his office. My finger slid down the list of As. *Not there. Lower. What the hell? A "B". I gave the list another look. Ah-hah! Two football players who never attended class got As.*

Anger welled up in my gut, and I stormed into Sigerseth's office without knocking. He looked up, wide-eyed, from a pile of papers, crushed his cigarette as if he didn't want me to know he was a smoker. I ranted; I got an "A" on the final. Why did I get a "B" in the course?"

Sigerseth's back straightened, as if there was a pipe running down his spine. "Burt, your grades were good, but I graded on a curve. Other students had higher totals."

I was confused. *This is the same guy who said he would take care of me. Now he beans me with a curve. Should I bitch about Jensen and Tully, the quarterback and halfback who got As and never attended class? No. Can't break the unwritten code: Never rat on another jock.*

Screwed, I walked out without saying another word. In the hall, Henry was gazing at the bulletin board. I wedged through a flock of students checking out their grades to tell him about Jensen and Tully.

After listening to my rant, he said, "They're projected to start next season. Football is king."

"What's baseball? Steerage?

"It's all about money."

Chapter 20

After venting my discontent to no avail, Henry and I exited the building and were hit by bright sunlight on the wide walkway. A short distance away, Charlie Franklin pulled up in the no parking zone in a green two-door '50 Chevy. He got out and approached us. There was no bounce to his step. He held an envelope in his hand and looked lost. Not the Charlie who thought he owned the town. Amidst a sea of students walking in every direction, Charlie spoke to Henry like he had just read his own obituary. "I got it," he said solemnly, and handed the envelope to Henry.

Henry fished out a letter and read in a muffled voice:

> *Dear Mr. Franklin,*
>
> *The University of Oregon regrets to inform you of a change in your status. Due to the fact that you have not made academic progress for a year-and-a-half, you have been dropped from the bachelor's degree program, effective immediately. In essence, you have flunked out.*
>
> *Regretfully,*
> *Austin Peabody*
> *Dean of Admission and Records*

Charlie, who appeared to be in shock, said, "They cut my scholarship after 26 games just like you said they would."

"What are you going to do now?"

"The Seattle Bakers called and asked me to play for them in the National AAU Tournament next month."

After a long beat, Henry asked, "How are you going to live until then? No apartment, no money, no food. How are you going pull that off?"

"I bought a 50-pound sack of potatoes. A friend said I could cook them at her place."

"Where are you going to sleep?"

Yesterday's hero studied his shoes. "Charlie will figure it out." With that he walked toward the P.E. entrance, past scores of students who had cheered for him last week, and now didn't acknowledge his presence.

Henry glanced at me. "I knew they would flunk him out. He hasn't taken his finals for a year-and-a-half."

We walked toward Mac Court as Henry continued. "This fuckin' place changed Charlie. He was a B+ student in high school and junior college. When he was admitted here they started taking care of him. Free apartment, free clothes, airfare to and from home, cash in his pocket. He started missing classes his first quarter. They covered for him. Then he didn't take his finals. They covered for him. Then he stopped going to school. They looked the other way."

"Until the season ended," I said.

"Yeah. The administration knew when his 26 games were over."

My mind spun. *First Padovan went down. Now Charlie. Who's next?*

Chapter 21

As I listened to Henry's chronology of Charlie's downfall, I spotted Otis several yards away, walking toward the arena entrance. "Hey, Otis!" I called out.

He turned, trying to match the voice with the face.

I waved. "Did you get your grades?"

He stopped and flashed a broad smile. "Yeah. I'm eligible."

"Where you goin'?" Henry asked suspiciously.

"Belko wants to see me."

"What about?"

"He didn't say."

"Meet us in the Jazz Room after dinner," Henry said, "and tell us what's up."

*   *   *

That night I entered the Jazz Room just as a drizzle turned into a downpour, drumming the windows and distorting the Platters rendition of "It's Twilight Time." I slid into a comfortable wingback chair just as Henry entered in wet gray sweats, looking like he was a victim of a flash flood. "Has Otis been here?" He had a sense of urgency in his voice and on his face.

"Not yet." *He's suspicious of something. But what?*

Henry was drawn to the hi-fi and immediately exchanged the record for Elvis' "I'm All Shook Up," a potential collector's item. He took the soft chair next to me, and said, "Elvis is going in the Army this month."

I said, "Bet they don't have room for his ten Cadillac convertibles," as Elvis sang, "Please don't ask me what's on my mind, I'm a little mixed up, but feeling fine."

Henry cracked open his textbook, then looked over. "I'm going to stay here during Spring break. I'm still on scholarship and I have a place to eat. How about you? Are you going south to play at Cal?"

I repositioned myself. "I've got a uniform, a travel bag and I'm excited. Kirsch told me I'm on the travel list. We're scheduled to play Portland State tomorrow if it's not rained out. I think that will have something to do with my scholarship."

A very different Otis entered the room. The joyous smile that displayed a full set of teeth had been replaced by a drawn face, downcast eyes, and slumped shoulders. He slipped off a very wet beige raincoat, tossed it on an open chair, and then plunked into a stuffed chair across from us and mumbled, "I talked to Belko."

Henry leaned forward. "What'd he say?"

"He cut my scholarship."

"I don't believe it!"

My stomach turned upside down as if I had just had a swig of rot-gut. *Belko screwed Otis by drawing a line through his name. He brought him a thousand miles for one season, and then cut him loose. Now arena applause is only going to be an echo in his mind.*

Otis sat motionless. The rain outside and the subject matter inside chilled the air. I didn't know if Otis was looking at us or through us. "Well, basketball is over," he said.

"Henry raised his voice. "This is pure horseshit."

Otis took a sharp breath and exhaled slowly, as if to slow himself down. "The only reason I came here was to play basketball. Now I'm four quarters from graduation and my scholarship money's gone."

I glanced at Henry. *The axe could have fallen on him as well. He broke curfew, broke a teammate's jaw, set a university record for stolen, long-play records. But he still had a tenuous scholarship.*

"What are you going to do?" I asked Otis.

Otis stared into space, like his brain had shut down. After a long beat, he said, "Coach Bowerman talked to me after I left Belko's office. He said he would pick up my scholarship if I high jumped for him." Otis shook his head. "I've never been out for track, don't know the first thing about high jumping. But if he thinks I can." He shook his head again. "I don't know." His voice trailed off.

I said nothing. *What do you say to a man who just got his heart cut out?*

Henry placed his hands on his kneecaps. "If you can high jump like you can dunk, you'll be great. Why don't you try it? My brother tied for the conference high jump title and he didn't have half the spring you have."

Rain continued to pound the windows as Otis sat silently, and I thought, *what does he do now—drop out of school, work at the lumber mill, return to Detroit and get a line job at Ford?*

Then all of sudden he said, "I'm going to give it a try. If this works I can high jump for two seasons and graduate." There was momentary silence before he added, "At least I won't wind up like Charlie."

"You're not going to wind up like Charlie," I blurted. "You never miss class and you take all your finals. How much time would you have before the first track meet?"

"I would have thirty days to learn how to high jump. Washington State is the first track meet."

"I think you can do it. I've seen you jump out of the gym when you dunk."

Otis gave me a thousand-yard stare, as if his mind was spinning faster that the record on the hi-fi.

"We'll be checking you out," I added.

"I have to get going," Henry said, pushing off his chair.

"Yeah. Me too. That's cool, Otis. A high jumper. I'll say I knew you when."

Henry and I left the student union together. The storm had cleared and stars flickered between the clouds. Streetlights reflected off the wet sidewalk, and our tennies sucked up water with each step. I inhaled cool, fresh air while branches of tall trees hanging over the sidewalk dripped cold water on my head. And I thought: *If there is one constant around here, it's change.*

Chapter 22

The next day, a crowned diamond that was thoroughly dry greeted me. Under a warm sun and great drainage, there wasn't a sign of dampness. And the grass had just been mowed. Perfect for baseball. Perfect for me to prove myself against Portland State.

In my white wool uniform with Kelly-green letters and numbers, I hustled at every opportunity in pregame drills to the tune of chatter like, "Way to go," "Atta boy," "Come to me big fella," and "You've got a great sausage for an arm." Encouragement and trash-talk that I completely welcomed. I even enjoyed the spitting of chewing tobacco from our first baseman, who juiced up the dusty, red clay soil around his bag. This was baseball.

Portland State players were dressed in rumpled gray uniforms with shrunken numerals and letters. When some of them warmed up, their arm actions were awkward, unlike the fluid throwing motions of our players. I wondered if there was any player on their squad that could make our team. After all, Oregon had taken the Northern Division of the Pacific Coast Conference the past five years.

By the time I was inserted into the lineup as the center fielder in the fifth inning, we were ahead six to two. The player I was competing with for my position moved to left field from center. About my size, he twisted his face and shook his head when he changed positions, indicating he was pissed. That was okay with me. It was my intention to get him real pissed off by beating him out.

From center field I could read the catcher's signals and react quickly to a hitter's swing, giving me the opportunity to get a jump on any hit ball in my area. I was more than ready. My senses were heightened on the first pitch, as well as my nose, which began to run. The longer I stayed in the outfield the worse my allergy became. I prayed the inning would end quickly.

The second batter hit a long drive to deep left-center. I knew immediately where it was going and how long it would take me to run it down. I hesitated to take off, wanting to make a sensational catch on the dead run, drawing the coach's attention to my speed. I was that good. And after some effort, I ran the ball down as planned for the second out. After I tossed the ball back to an infielder, I indicated two outs to the left fielder, by flashing two fingers, a procedural thing for the center fielder to do. Strangely, he reciprocated with a raised index finger, telling me there was only one out. I thought, *if that jerk wants to look stupid, let him. Maybe the coach will see the guy can't count.*

After the next hitter grounded out to end the inning, everyone in the field sprinted toward the dugout except the left fielder, who now thought there were two outs. When I reached the infield grass, I looked back; he was still standing out there as if the inning wasn't over. Then he ran after the pack, flashing a dirty look in my direction.

At the plate, I flew out to deep right field twice. I also made a diving catch of a sinking line drive near the left field wall, and I didn't get paralyzed, something that could happen by knocking down a defensive player, or running into the wall.

I came out better than my competition, who grounded out meekly four times.

After the game, our squad sat on the cement stands, as the coach read names on the travel roster aloud. Everything was riding on the sound of my name, a trip to Cal, a scholarship, my career. I held my breath and waited as the coach went down the alphabet. Then he read my name. I took a deep breath and a feeling of exhilaration came over me.

Several minutes later, in our cramped locker room below the basketball court, players smiled at each other. Some shook hands. Sitting on a wood bench, I felt like a heavy weight had just been removed from my shoulders. I looked over at Kirsch, who stood near the door talking with an older man. The man was balding, had a very white face, and wore a half-buttoned green golf sweater.

Kirsch pointed in my direction. Neither man smiled. Then Kirsch worked his way through half-dressed players to tell me that he wanted to see me in his office.

Probably about my scholarship, I thought.

About a half-hour later, Kirsch sat behind his desk, fiddling with a pen as he spoke rapidly to me. He had opened with, "It was a nice catch you made today."

Sitting on the other side of his desk, anxious to hear about my scholarship, I smiled and thanked him. Then he said, "The Athletic Director, Leo Harris, came to see me today."

The middle-aged guy in the locker room.

"I don't know how to break this to you, so I'll give it to you straight. You're ineligible."

His words were like a blow to my head. Trying to recover, I said, "I passed all my classes and carried a full load. I am eligible."

He delivered another blow with, "You don't have enough credits between quarters. You didn't go to school last fall. You need twenty-four semester units to be eligible. You had sixteen."

I hammered back, "I was sick last fall. Dropped out of school. But I passed all sixteen units last spring and I sent you my JC transcript. Didn't you look at it?"

Dead silence, before Kirsch said, "I'm sorry, we should have picked it up. We can't do anything now. You'll just have to wait for next year."

One moment I was on top of the world, the next moment I had no world. *There is no next year. My pro career is cancelled. Can't sign a contract at twenty-three. Not enough time to go all the way. I'd wind up being just another minor league player.*

Badly wounded, I left his office without saying another word. Spring break had begun, and I wandered through an empty campus, mourning the death of baseball. I kept walking, oblivious to everything except baseball—what I had lived for since elementary school.

The setting sun blinding me, I found myself at the Willamette River, miles from campus. There I stood on the sandy shoreline and watched the water rush by as random thoughts continued to dart through my head. *I've come a long way. Played with the threat of paralysis, fourteen sprained ankles. Came back from being a washout in high school and community college to make all-league and all-conference. Is this all there is?*

What do I do? Quit Oregon? Get a job like Dad said? Work for a menial wage? That's not me.

My mind rewound, and I recalled what got me this far—a significant ah-hah moment in my life. I had been drifting as a high school student/ athlete, marked for failure. My father, who sold furniture, TVs, and appliances door-to-door in Boyle Heights and its periphery to people who had no credit, was bedridden for months with something no doctor had an explanation for. Part of his job was to make weekly collections from his customers who slowly paid off their debt. With no household income, I took it upon myself to make his collections on weekends, using his car, going into neighborhoods where the brave dared not go, stuffing my pockets with cash, and hoping to hell to get out before dark. Then I got the bright idea that I needed to bring in more money to the house and got a delivery job clear across the city in West L.A. for $.75 an hour. The only hitch was that I had to use my father's car and cut my fourth, fifth, and sixth period classes, which I did. Education had little value, so why not, I thought.

After two months on the afternoon job, I was driving home on the freeway from work about 5:30 in the afternoon on a hot, sticky day, when I was trapped in Civic Center traffic. Locked in for several minutes, listening to my engine grind away, I looked over at the shiny new car to my right. There, a guy wearing a white shirt and tie, sat quietly behind the wheel, his windows up. He had A/C. Rare in the mid-fifties.

Then it hit me. *The guy has an expensive new car, nice clothes, and probably a great job, a college education, and a great self-image. What do*

I have? No education, old clothes, little money, little self-respect. "Shit," I mumbled. I'd like to be that guy . . . But my life is going nowhere! I've been pretending it was going somewhere . . . If I don't change right now I'll be trying to survive at some menial job for the rest of my life.

When traffic loosened up, and my old Chevy rolled slowly forward, I decided to quit my afternoon job, go back to school and be a different person. Putting pretention to work, I decided to walk, talk, and act like the person and the baseball player I envisioned myself to be. A step in the right direction. I went back to school, earned As, got involved with school activities, and began to improve my baseball playing, all because I left my other self on the freeway that day.

*   *   *

I picked up a small rock and tossed it across the river with everything I had. *The arm is still there. But I'm not.* I felt a chill in the air and in my bones. Across the river, the sun dipped below the pine trees, and their long shadows started to darken the water. I began the long walk back to campus, trudging up a sandy path to the roadway. *If I'm not a baseball player, who am I? Competing in baseball is all I know . . . I planned to coach after baseball, but I didn't think it would come so soon . . . Two more years I can coach. Not like Kirsch . . . What's mom going to say? She always introduced me as "Burt the baseball player."*

Sorrow turned to anger as I stepped onto the sidewalk that was a straightaway to campus. I was pissed at Oregon, pissed at the NCAA rulebook, pissed at Kirsch. Then reality raised its ugly head. *I'm stuck. Have to return for the spring quarter and progress toward a degree, then transfer. It's April. Oregon is on the quarter system. Semester systems will start up again in L.A. in September . . . I'm broke. No money for round trip bus ride to L.A. to raise money for food, lodging, tuition. Not enough gas money . . . I have $3,000 in a trust fund coming in May from the auto accident. But what do I do now?*

Chapter 23

Depressed, I gathered my clothes to move out of the dorm and store them in my car. *Maybe hitchhike to San Francisco, then hop on a bus for L.A. Leave my car at Henry's house with all my belongings in the trunk. But I don't know if I'm coming back.*

Aki, my ex-roommate, watched me carefully pack. "Ever been to San Francisco?" he asked.

What's he thinking? "Last summer. I didn't see everything I wanted to see. I was visiting Cal Berkeley, then went into the city. That's what they call it—the city. I was there for a few hours. Why?"

"I'm driving there with my friend this afternoon."

"Great place, San Francisco! You'll love it! Mind if I ride along with you? From San Francisco, I can get on a bus to L.A. and go home."

"Okay. But L.A. is a long way. Are you coming back here?"

"I don't have an answer to that right now."

*   *   *

Sitting in the back seat as Aki drove south on 99, I gazed at the extensive lineup of pine trees along the highway, trying to figure out how I could get enough money to return to school. I was lucky to hitch a ride with Aki and his friend, another student from Japan whom my roommate used to hang out with. And I was betting my luck would hold out.

Aki glanced in his rearview mirror and spoke to me about his favorite TV show, *Gun Smoke*. He was enamored with cowboys because they didn't have any in Japan, and the show was one of his favorite topics. As we sped by a large lake, he talked about each character, finally concluding miles later with, "I make cowboy movies for Japanese television."

"Where are you going to film?"

Aki shook his head and went on to share his concept of a record player in each Japanese car that he was going to import to the states. Ideas popped in and out of his head like kernels of corn heating up in a popcorn machine.

"Is the record player going to be in the glove compartment?" I asked.

"Small records. Small machine."

"Wouldn't the needle jump every time you went over a pothole?"

Aki, who had an answer for every situation, said, "Not in my car."

Several miles later, Aki ran out of ideas, and I turned to watch the scenery fly by. From Eugene to Ashland the snow was melting beneath tall pines and the earth was dark and spotted with ferns. Thoughts surfaced, then disappeared. *I missed Joan. It would be good to see her again. She wouldn't get my situation. Nobody would. I still had the quarter I used to call her on the rigged payphone every other week. What am I going to tell my parents? Do I have war bonds from World War II left? Mom took care of that.*

As we passed the Ashland turnoff, it dawned on me that because I dropped out of school last fall, I would have been ineligible for baseball at any university I transferred to. And no baseball coach who was recruiting me said anything about that fact. *Doesn't anyone read transcripts?*

We crossed the Oregon border into California. Double yellow lines in the middle of the highway became double white lines, the clouds opened up and a warm sun peeked through. I leaned back, placed my head on the seat, shut my eyes and tried to catch some z's. But I thought about my friends at Oregon who were either dropped from their scholarships (like me) or suspended.

*   *   *

When we arrived at the old San Francisco bus depot, I climbed aboard a Greyhound, took a soft seat and fell asleep within minutes. After an all-nighter in the packed bus, I awoke on the Hollywood Freeway, closing in on downtown Hollywood, and about a half hour from home. I reached back, pulled out my wallet and counted my reserves for the tenth time. I had food money for a month, enough for a return bus ride to Eugene, plus twenty bucks for incidentals. All I needed was five hundred more.

I gazed at the round Capital Records building, the first identifiable building I saw in southern California. *An old friend. Home to Hollywood, the transplanted Dodgers . . . and your fuckin' baseball career is over.*

My stomach turned. The wound was still raw.

The bus kept rolling past Hollywood, on its way to downtown Los Angeles. And I thought: *Forget about it . . . Go on . . . You're embarrassed. When you left L.A. you were somebody . . . A guy with a scholarship on his way to a big-time university and a baseball career . . . Your picture was in the paper . . . Now you have a lot of explaining to do.*

That afternoon, in our living room, I confessed my misgivings to my parents, as they sat back on a gray sofa for two that was fitted with a clear plastic cover that supposedly guaranteed the furniture's longevity. Sitting across from them in a folding chair, I told my mother about my situation. I didn't look at my father, for I knew he would have no compassion. He had discarded the idea of being a pharmacist, dropped out of CCNY, got married, and somehow survived the Depression, then built ships at Bethlehem Steel during the war. My mother, a short woman with an explosive temper wrapped in a calm exterior, nodded with understanding. She always felt empathy for me when I was in trouble, except when I was in trouble with her.

My father tore into the conversation with, "Now that you're finished with baseball, you can get a job. That's what we do. We work."

I shuddered at the thought of being unqualified for a decent job. I had worked entry-level at U.S. Steel the past summer, a job that dulled my brain and my hearing for little compensation. I sawed hydraulic aluminum tubes all day, until I was fired for slowing down while I was thinking what a stupid job this was. I needed to compete in this world using my brain.

I looked into my mother's eyes. "I want to return to Oregon this week. And I need five hundred bucks for tuition and room and board." I took a long, hopeful breath. "My war bonds. How much do I have left?"

"That went for your Bar Mitzvah party years ago," she said softly.

"How about stocks?"

"The only investment we have is in this house."

"Can I get a bank loan?"

Her eyes narrowed. "Did you meet some curvaceous cutie at Oregon? Is that why you want to go back?"

"No. Mom, I just want to move forward with my education. And I can't transfer to a college down here until September."

She glanced at the adjacent kitchen, and peeled away from the plastic wrapped sofa. "You've got no collateral, but I'll see what I've got."

She doesn't have anything.

My father got up, turned on the twelve-inch black-and-white TV and disappeared from the conversation as he always did when my mother took charge, which was frequently.

I followed my mother into the kitchen where white appliances and a small chrome-rimmed dinette set sat occupying a cramped space. She reached as high as her 5' 1" frame would take her, deep into the second shelf of the cabinet, and brought down a sugar bowl. Then she turned it over on the table. A large roll of bills dropped out—money she probably squirrelled away for years from my father's meager income. She looked into my eyes and, I felt, spoke with a heavy heart. "I had to quit school in the eighth grade," she said, "to take care of my brothers and sisters. I was the oldest of seven. I made sure they all graduated from high school. When your grandfather bought the bathhouse in Brooklyn, he sent me to a business school to learn accounting. I never got the education I wanted. There was always something else going on in my life. Now I want you to make it all the way." She handed me the roll. "You'll be the first one in our family to get a degree. There's two-fifty here. This isn't enough for all your bills. You still have to hash for meals and you're going to have to figure out how to get a room, but I trust you can do that."

I blinked back tears, took a hard to come-by breath. "Somehow I'll go all the way. And I'll pay you back. Next month, on my twenty-first birthday, I'll be eligible to get my trust fund . . . And I'll pay you back when I get home in June. My bank doesn't have offices in Oregon."

"You worked all summer when you were fifteen to buy our oven. We're even."

I slid the bills in my pocket, and gave my mother a big hug. Then a queasy feeling set in as the "anything is possible" attitude left me. I had no idea how I was going to get a room with no money.

Chapter 24

That afternoon, I drove my father's car to Joan's house in nearby Montebello, my mind playing back what her mother told me back in December—*If you leave, your relationship with Joan will be over. I tried to keep the relationship alive with long-distance phone calls. Called her when I got home. But her voice seemed distant, like her mother was right.* I kept driving, hoping I was wrong.

During our visit, I found that my vibes were on the mark. Instead of catching up by going out to a movie followed by a hamburger and a coke, or walking around the block and talking about how much I missed her, or that I was transferring to Cal State L.A., or sharing my predicament, my damaged ego, or my loss of identity, I made superficial conversation as Joan ironed vacation wear in preparation for joining her girlfriends on Balboa Island in Orange County that afternoon. Another rejection. A depressive reality. *I was losing a girlfriend to an island. Jesus, give me a blindfold and a cigarette before pulling the trigger.* My mind continued to spin as we continued inane conversation. *Balboa Island! Easter Week! . . . Where college students go for a wild week! . . . Not the girl I thought I knew . . . Only a high school junior and going to Devil's Island . . . Got to be more to this . . . Her mother was right. It's over . . . You left her, now she's leaving you . . .* But baseball was calling.

* * *

The next day, I called my old friend Ernie Rodriguez. Having performed well in the Canadian College Summer League, he landed a scholarship at UCLA and was now starring on their baseball team, just as he had planned. He said he was going to lead the conference in hitting. I asked him how he liked UCLA and he said the most difficult thing was finding a place to park. But he figured out that he could park on Westwood Boulevard in front of the old Men's Gym and leave an "out of gas" sign on the window. He had been doing that for months. Always an angle for people from the Heights.

The next day, I borrowed my father's car again and made the long drive across L.A. to Westwood and the UCLA campus. A smile crossed my face as I passed Central Market in downtown L.A. on my way to turning west on Wilshire Boulevard, and I thought back to when Ernie and I had to stop there when we were kids to get our bearings.

We were sixth graders, and baseball nuts, playing baseball every day, following the major league box scores of our favorite players in the paper, listening to re-created games on the radio, and in the interim, playing a two-man game at Sheridan Street Playground where there was only a pitcher and a hitter.

As I turned right onto Wilshire Boulevard and headed for Westwood and the distant UCLA campus, I thought about how much time and effort I had put in to become a baseball player, and that I was chasing a dream that had turned into a nightmare.

* * *

The UCLA baseball field was on campus next to the track where Jackie Robinson set long jump records in 1940. Sitting in the packed stands on a hard bench seat that sunny day, I noticed basketball Coach John Wooden and his assistant Jerry Norman sitting one row below me. Nice job, coaching basketball and having the time to enjoy a ballgame. *Something I'd like to do some day if I knew more about that game.* Another thought surfaced when I inhaled a mix of freshly cut grass, and ocean air coming in from Santa Monica. It was the camaraderie of teammates and the competition under pressure that I missed. Not the elements of pressure I was under now, but another situation where everything is dependent on me.

Watching the teams warm up, I recalled being in a body-cast during my junior year of high school to repair the crack in my spine. That cast was heavy, made my movements awkward, and made me look like Frankenstein. I knew when it was made for me that I would miss a varsity baseball season. I concluded that without baseball there was no reason to go to school. So I stopped going to school. And as December drifted into January, I continued to sit in my bathrobe in the breakfast nook and play the horses, without money of course. And after a month, I was up $1200. But I was at ground zero with my mother. She finally took me to see a shrink. I don't remember where this guy hung his shingle, or how we got to his office. I only remember a brief exchange before the guy said to me, "The trouble is you have all your chickens in one basket."

I quickly replied, "I only have one basket."

That didn't go over well, so my mother brought my baseball coach to our house, a man I was afraid of—Coach Campolo who ended my hold-out with, "If you don't go to school tomorrow, I'm coming to get you."

*   *   *

The crack of the bat brought me back. Ernie was the next batter. As he strolled to the batter's box, I applauded him. He was one tough competitor. He took two pitches and lined a shot to right field. A single. And I thought, *Man, I'd love to do that again. I can still play semi-pro ball on weekends for the gas money while I sit out a year. My resume would look good when I apply for a coaching job. But it's going to be a long wait.*

Chapter 25

After a lengthy bus ride, I arrived at the Eugene depot on a cloudy Friday morning, three days before spring quarter began. Henry picked me up in my car. He was taking good care of it, like it was his. It was washed, and a short stack of long-play records was nestled in the back seat. I stowed my luggage along with Sinatra and Elvis in the trunk and told Henry to get rid of those damn records.

He said nothing. I guessed that was a "no."

I drove toward campus listening to Henry report that he had had no luck finding me a bed, and the empty feeling I'd had many times during the last quarter returned. And as we rolled past quiet residential streets toward campus, my feeling of being hollowed increased, and I thought about the people I didn't want to be like. One was my Boyle Heights neighbor, Louie, who dreamed of owning an auto parts store. For years, he would bring home car parts and toss them into his one-car garage in back of our duplex. It became floor-to-ceiling engines, bumpers, radios, wires, hoods. A mass of disorganization for some future date, which never came.

* * *

I pulled up to the Student Union to sit down with Henry over a cup of tea and devise a plan B, although we had never really had a plan A.

Henry was worried that if I didn't get a bed, I would take my car and go home, making it impossible for him to travel to his student teaching assignment many miles from campus. He didn't know that somehow, someway, I was going to complete the spring quarter, and that my greatest fear was not being homeless, but being stuck my whole life like my former neighbor.

We took seats in the crowded, glassed-in Student Union food service area. I stared into the darkness of my five-cent cup of tea as Henry and I threw out ideas: sleep on a student union couch, sleep in my car, sleep on a park bench. Then Henry waved a hand. "There's got to be someone who wants a roommate and won't charge you."

"How am I going to find that person?"

"I know every jock on campus," Henry said, covering his mouth with a hand, then bursting out in laughter. "Maybe Bob Heard wants a roommate."

"Screw you, too! The football coach probably keeps him in a cage. Heard might be a great player, but he hates people. Can you imagine? I blocked his punch and the son of a bitch still knocked me out. I'd rather sleep in my car."

"I'll ask around."

*   *   *

With my mother's words, "You'll be the first one in our family to get a degree," ringing in my head, coupled with the thought of collecting car parts all my life, I paid my tuition after sleeping in my car for three nights. Like Cortez, I had burnt all my ships in the harbor. Now there was no turning back. Then I had a passing thought. *If Cortez was a fuckin' wacko, what am I?*

Unfortunately, I had to scrounge up meals for a couple of days, and I had to shower and shave in the P.E. locker room, using the towels I brought from home. I would place the towels under my Chevy's back window, roll all my windows up and hope that the sun would come out, and the interior would heat up, creating a makeshift clothes dryer.

On Sunday morning, after a cup-of-tea breakfast, I crossed paths with Charlie Franklin in the hallway of the union. Yesterday's star looked like hell. Rumpled clothes, three-week beard, eyes sunk into his head. Looking for a better answer to my own accommodations, I asked him where he was sleeping. He pointed at a nearby couch.

Feeling like Charlie looked, I said, "I'm sleeping in my car."

"The couch is better," he said in low voice, as if he had been in solitary for months. "Nobody checks."

With a stream of students passing us and paying no attention to whatever had became of Charlie, I asked him, "When are you going to play for the Seattle Bakers in the AAU nationals?"

"Couple of weeks. Then I'll be eating steak."

"What are you going to do after that?"

He shrugged. "Maybe they'll give me a job."

"Good luck."

"Thanks, 'Ol Fade."

As I walked away, I thought, *I haven't fallen into the Oregon abyss yet, but I'm close.*

* * *

That evening, preparing to spend another miserable night in my car, I sipped hot tea in the Student Union, waiting for Henry. He appeared as scheduled, slid into a chair, smiled and said over the crowd noise with enthusiasm, "I have a lead for you, man. A football player from Portland said he's got a friend living in the all-male frosh dorm that doesn't have a roommate and wants one. It's inevitable. You're going to get a bed."

"Nothing's inevitable until it happens."

"Hang in there." Henry glanced over his right shoulder at the clock high above the buffet counter. "The guy's meeting us here in a few minutes."

"I hope so. My body is a pretzel."

Henry gazed at the entrance, a short distance away. "I don't know what the guy looks like. But his name is Ivan." Henry stood and faced the entrance. "I heard that the guy saw me play and knows my face."

A flock of noisy coeds wearing typical long-sleeve, wool sweaters and pleated skirts entered and exited. Then three guys sauntered in. A big guy munching a donut, a little guy with thick glasses and a propeller cap, and a tall guy with slicked black hair wearing a beige raincoat. The first guy headed for the buffet. The second guy made a beeline for a frat group that was raising hell in a far corner. The third guy pointed at Henry and came our way.

I smiled a nervous smile.

After introductions, we settled into the hard chairs and talked in conspiratorial tones. Ivan, who appeared to be a straight-laced guy, spoke to me as if we were old friends, making me feel welcome. He'd been out of high school for six months and just enrolled. He confirmed that he was never assigned a roommate and said he was tired of talking to the walls. Not wanting to bore him with my problems, I only told him that I was a junior, not a freshman. Ivan didn't blink. "I've got plenty of room," he said.

"Great. When can I move in?"

"Any time."

I thought out loud about the negative ramifications of the move, something I should have kept to myself. "You understand," I said in a hushed tone, "that I'll be a phantom resident, a junior living in a frosh-only dorm. If the university finds out, I'll have to pay a big bill and I'm broke. What's more, you'd be a co-conspirator."

Henry gave me a hard look. "You talk like you've got choices."

"I just want to clear the air."

"Just be invisible," Ivan said, signaling the adventure to begin.

*   *   *

At midnight, I quietly moved my belongings into Ivan's second floor room, which was just across the hall from the stairwell. The dorm was a year old and had the scent of fresh laundry with a hint of varnish. I carefully laid a stack of clothes on the unoccupied bed as Ivan read a

Sports Illustrated magazine with a cover photo of a Milwaukee catcher named Del Crandall. "I really appreciate this." I looked around. "Larger than my last place. And you've got heat coming from a ceiling vent. Better than steam pipes."

"Sh-sh-sh. Keep it down. The walls are thin."

My heart jacked when I opened the door a crack. I had three or four more trips to make. The hallway was clear. I turned back and said quietly, "Keep the door unlocked. I have a few more trips. And get me a key to the room."

"Be careful."

In the silence of the night, it took me three more trips to haul my clothes up the stairs and safely into Ivan's room. On my last trip, just as I opened the stairwell door, I saw a guy in skivvies scurrying down the hall in my direction. I clicked the door shut and listened closely, hoping he was headed to the communal bathroom. When I thought I heard a door shut, I shot across the hall with my belongings.

* * *

Staying invisible at the frosh dorm wasn't easy, but I developed a schedule that worked for a while. I would get up at 5:30, clean up and leave the dorm by 6:00 before the freshmen were up, just in time to serve breakfast to them on the other side of the building. At night, I would return to the room after 11:30 when I guessed everyone on the floor was asleep. I studied in the library until 10:00, then had a cup of tea in the union with Henry until 11:15. I would catch up on my sleep in the library or student union couch in the afternoon, cutting short my study time but reviving myself so I could go on.

113

Chapter 26

I kept everyone except Henry at arm's length during the quarter, fearing discovery of my living arrangements. Consequently, I only had surface conversations with faculty and students that never went past, "How's it going?" or "Can't complain."

Otis Davis wasn't privy to my situation, although he was in my Kinesiology and Organization and Administration of P.E. courses. Otis, now a member of the track team, was not in Methods of Coaching Track and Field with me. There, Coach Bowerman, the guy who told me to walk pigeon-toed, was the instructor.

I didn't have enough money to buy an eight-dollar Kinesiology text, but thought that with a little luck I could pass that class without the professor ever knowing I missed reading assignments. I probably could have borrowed Otis's book, but I had too much pride to discuss my financial situation with him.

Although I was still upset with Dr. Sigerseth's approach to grading no-shows, I enrolled in his spring course, Organization and Administration of P.E., thinking it was too interesting to pass up.

On the first day of class, I wore a wool sweater over a white-T-shirt and pressed khakis that I ironed very late at night in the frosh dorm laundry area. I was in style, your common everyday look. And no one would ever think I was really the phantom.

I sat in the front row ready to take copious notes, Otis in the next chair. Dr. Sigerseth welcomed us, and then said, "Soon you will be student teaching and applying for teaching and coaching jobs. Those of you who have been coasting through this major need to get more serious and listen closely to what I have to say. These are the kinds of things you have to do now: listen, take notes, do well on tests and the class project."

I'm not going to graduate from this fuckin' place. But I will be coaching baseball . . . Maybe playing somewhere . . . No, that's over . . . No, it's not . . . Yes, it's over.

After making a hash mark on my paper when Sigerseth said, "These are the kinds of things." I raised my hand. "Is it true that when we apply for a teaching job, we have to swear that we're not communists?"

"Yes. These are the kinds of things that are on the application," the professor said, while standing over Otis, oblivious to his adding another checkmark to the top of his page.

"I don't even know what a communist is," I said.

"I've heard you are one," blurted Otis, who got a chuckle from a few students.

"If I were a communist," I said to Sigerseth, "I wouldn't tell the school district."

"These are the kinds of things that exist. I can't change them. Now let's move on to the class project."

He went on to explain that each of us was to develop an entire physical education plant on paper: gyms, fields, lockers, and offices, including architectural drawings down to the floor joists in the gym.

I looked around at the looks of acceptance on the faces in the packed room, thinking that it was a very ambitious project for a three-unit class—really for an advanced degree. But by the end of class I decided to create something very special. I had an idea.

Chapter 27

Coach Bowerman taught Methods of Coaching Track and Field, a prerequisite for graduation in my major. The class was held right after lunch and attended by a bunch of football players looking for an easy grade, and one outsider, me. The room was dusty and bare bones.

In our first session, Bowerman demonstrated how to properly release a sixteen-ounce shot put. In front of his desk, a few feet from the first row where I sat, he placed the heavy iron ball into his hand and behind his right ear. Then he turned his back to the students, bent at the waist and knees, and suddenly uncoiled and heaved the shot toward the big guy sitting next to me. The iron ball appeared to move in slow motion toward the student who was frozen in place, as was I. Then the shot hit the guy's chest and fell to the floor. But it wasn't a shot at all. It was a softball. Bowerman had heaved a damn softball. Like magic, somewhere in Bowerman's motion, he had exchanged the shot for a softball.

Bowerman broke out in laughter. All the students laughed, except the guy who was the butt of the joke. I sat there and thought: *Anything is possible with this guy.*

During the next class, Bowerman discussed the creation and manufacture of new running shoes and running surfaces. He went into detail about how he was creating these products. On this day, he had brought a thin soled, black leather track shoe to class that he had dissected lengthwise. When he held the shoe up, I could see that the skin on his palm had flaked dramatically, as if he had a horrible fungus infection. But when he spoke about gluing the shoe parts together I thought his affliction was probably dried glue on his skin.

Bowerman gave us a look like he was ready to take the beach, and said, "I am going to improve the track shoe. When I do, we will jump higher and run faster. I've been melting down tires with my wife's waffle irons to make new soles." He paused to take a breath. "Thus far, I've ruined nine waffle irons, but I'm close to something . . . I know it."

Although I recognized that the classroom was Bowerman's playground, and we weren't going to learn a damn thing about track and field, after class I offered to help this futurist as a student assistant for his track workouts a few days a week. Bowerman was an idea guy, and I was always drawn to idea people. When I was growing up, I was into authors like Jules Verne, and Alexander Dumas, and warrior Lawrence of Arabia. In high school, my basketball coach Blaine Crowther, who found ways to win despite being the underdog, also impressed me. I had time now. I thought I could learn something that I could apply to the game of baseball. And I could also watch Bowerman reinvent Otis as a high jumper.

Chapter 28

For the next couple of weeks, as an unpaid assistant to Bowerman, I watched Otis Davis attempt to perfect his high jump technique at aged Hayward Field, an expandable ten thousand-seat facility used for football and track events. When Bowerman had a free moment, I would question him about proper arm and leg movement for sprinting. Although I was quick on my feet, I thought I could be better.

Early in the season, a misty 40-degree afternoon wind made it difficult to warm up for an entire week. But Otis, the lone Black guy on the team, was not deterred, and continued to train outside every day, followed Bowerman's directions, and was the last athlete to leave the field.

Unfortunately, the spring Otis had demonstrated on the basketball court did not translate into a winning high jump performance. After two weeks, a six-foot jump was all he could muster, and Bowerman told him that he would need to clear 6 feet 6 inches to have a chance at placing third in conference meets—which meant keeping his scholarship his final year. Talk about pressure!

A week later, on another cold afternoon, when shadows filled the field, I stood next to the high jump in my overcoat and watched Otis practice as sprinters, distance runners, hurdlers, pole vaulters and weight men all went through their paces. A three-ring circus. And there was Otis, trying to cross over the bar face down. But time after time his trail leg nicked the crossbar, causing it to spring up, quiver and fall to the matted sawdust pit. Repeatedly, Otis would get to his knees and look quizzically at the toppled crossbar. Then he'd pound the sawdust pit in disgust, dust himself off and replace the bar carefully on its mountings. This time he walked back, rechecked his take-off marks, looked at me and snarled, "Well, aren't you going to say something?"

"Yeah. Coach Bowerman wants you to run some wind sprints with the pole vaulters and hurdlers at the south goal line in a couple of minutes."

"More fun than this."

"You're close to solving the mystery of your event. It'll probably come tomorrow. Hang in there."

"Let's go! Wind sprints!" Bowerman yelled from the far end of the field.

Minutes later, athletes lined up, then reacted to Bowerman shouting the word "Go." Large groups of athletes in dark green hooded sweatshirts sprinted a hundred yards on grass, jogged back to the goal line from which they came, then sprinted again. I stood at the finish line and timed Otis as he consistently beat the field by ten yards.

After the last sprint, I ran back to Bowerman holding up my watch. "Coach, I've got Otis with all ten flat times."

Bowerman twisted his face. "You probably have the broken watch."

"Maybe, but he just ran ten sprints with little recovery and while everyone else is gasping for air he still has gas in his tank."

Bowerman stared at me with an expression that could turn milk sour. He was good at that. "Well," he said, "he can't high jump. He better be good at something."

It wasn't difficult to interpret Bowerman's words, but I didn't mention the coach's position to Otis as we walked across an empty field toward the locker rooms. He needed a miracle in a hurry.

Chapter 29

Instead of buying an eight-dollar Kinesiology textbook, I used the money to buy four Sunday dinners when the cafeteria was closed. I thought Professor Goddard would never catch on since his mimeographed handouts and lecture notes were carrying me through his tests. However, a month into the course, the professor said, "Burt, how would you handle problem number 5?"

Sitting high up in the bleacher-type seating arrangement, my heart in my mouth, I eyed the tabletop and said nothing, waiting for him to call on someone else. With all eyes on me, Goddard, who always wore a colorful sweater and slacks, said, "Burt, that's problem 5 on page 20. Are you with me?"

I squeezed out, "I don't have a book, sir." I waited for his reaction.

Goddard's eyebrows pinched. "See me after class."

It was the kind of meeting I feared. It could mean discovery and room eviction. When the room had cleared after class, I spoke to Goddard at the door.

"Why don't you have a book?" he asked.

"I can't afford one."

Goddard looked at me for a long moment, then said, "I'll buy you one. I have an account at the bookstore. Where do you live? I'll pick you up?"

A gut punch. Come to my dorm? No way. "Uh, I live in town. But I'm on campus all day. I'll meet you at the bookstore."

"Okay. Bookstore at four."

Late that afternoon, I waited for the professor at the bookstore checkout counter thinking how much I liked Kinesiology, the study of athletic motion. I had learned which muscles needed to be developed to swing a bat and throw a baseball with major league strength, information that I needed to be a successful coach. But I was aware that at any time I could expose my phantom status.

A young man about my size, who wore an Oregon baseball cap over tufts of black curls, purchased a book at the counter and came my way. I recognized him as the freshman who always wanted me to pile extra bacon on his scrambled eggs. He nodded. I nodded back, then looked in the distance avoiding conversation. Just then, the professor strutted toward me. "Burt, here's the book. It's good. I wrote it. Now you can answer problem number 5. I'll look forward to you handing in a one-page answer at our next class."

I thanked him. But I was embarrassed. I hated handouts. The book in my hand, I stood near the counter visualizing an eight-year-old kid receiving a holiday gift. I was at the free clinic where I received asthma treatments. I was in front of a table loaded with toys, eyeing a box that contained miniature bricks to build your own house. "Free," someone said. "Take the box. It's free." I knew what it was all about. I took the box. And I felt like shit.

Chapter 30

The weather had warmed and the air was still as I scurried to the library after dinner. My luck had held up, and in broad daylight I had managed to avoid all freshmen on the second floor of the dorm for four weeks. Good for an introvert, but difficult for me. I was normally friendly with everyone. But this was not normal. For me, there was no normal.

The library was ornate, rectangular, and in good condition for its years. The one-level building consisted of a large study hall with spotless, oversized tables, crammed bookshelves that ran up four walls, and stacks covering half the room. In the center of the room was an information kiosk.

I was anxious to research existing physical education facilities and create a unique physical education plant. Something new, uncommon. Upon entering, I took a seat across from Henry near the exit of the quiet room, hoping that he wouldn't say something funny that would cause us to break out laughing and get thrown out. The librarian had warned us several times already.

While doodling on three-hole lined paper, I came up with the idea for a domed stadium to fulfill the class project requirement. Thinking that a doomed facility had already been created and that I could copy one, maybe expand on the concept, I went to see the librarian. "Excuse me," I said quietly to the middle-aged woman with hair pulled back in a bun. "I'm looking for information about athletic field houses, roofed football fields, stuff like that."

I got a "what-the-hell-is-that" look. "Try the periodicals, *Coach* and *Scholastic Coach*, in the stacks. You might find something there."

In the stacks I found bound issues of those magazines dating back ten years. I took all I could carry to my table and thumbed through years of those periodicals and learned that an increasing number of universities in the Midwest were building field houses that contained half a football field, with a low ceiling, on a dirt surface. Not what I had in mind.

It was apparent that I had to create something new that Sigerseth would probably think was bizarre. Minutes passed as I sat quietly and considered if I should dig in and develop something that might not be acceptable. But the challenge wouldn't leave my mind. And I had a history of not letting go of an idea until I had beaten it to death. That's why I was still in Oregon.

As the clock on the wall ticked down toward closing time, I worked feverishly to come up with a drawing that seemed feasible. I didn't want to construct a building with half an idea. With all gears on full, I outlined the top view of a football field, then added a 330-yard running track with six lanes around the field. Then I outlined a basketball court on top of the field. Then came coaches' offices, men's and women's locker facilities, wrestling, dance and weight-lifting rooms beyond the end zone and far curve of the track. On another piece of paper I placed a portable basketball floor to be placed as needed on the football field. That floor could also be used for volleyball and badminton. I continued to draw in tall rows of permanent bleachers that edged up to the track along with sets of portable bleachers that could roll out over the track for a football or basketball game. The stands would hold 20,000 fans. To complete my concept, I drew a front view of the complex with a large roof that covered the towering walls.

Then I took another look at it and recognized that I had just expanded and covered my high school football field. "Not a bad idea," I mumbled to myself.

"Let's see what you've got," Henry said.

I handed over my scribbles. He examined my work and said in a hushed tone, "This is no high school P.E. facility," Henry said, as he picked it apart. "Too large. Too expensive. Sigerseth won't dig it. Why do you need a roof, anyway?"

"So you can hold a football or basketball game or track meet in any weather. And also have a basketball arena. One facility for all sports takes up less space. You don't have to build a football stadium and a separate gym."

"How are you going to hold up the roof without having posts in the stands?"

I sat back. "I have no fuckin' idea."

"And grass can't grow inside. Come on."

"Never thought of that. But, hey I'm just starting."

Henry added, "Even Ruben Toolbox couldn't invent indoor grass."

I tried to control myself, failed and burst out laughing. "Who is Ruben Toolbox?"

"Sh-sh-sh," Came the muffled urging from students at the next table.

In compliance, Henry lowered his voice. "Ruben Toolbox is nobody 'cause he couldn't invent indoor grass."

"I'm just going to let my ideas flow. You've got to take a risk now and then."

"Well, you certainly know how to do that," he said, as he slid back my work.

Henry, whose mind was always cranking, scanned the library and a smile crossed his face. "Hey, Burt, we need some projects to break the boredom. No basketball, no baseball, no pressure. We need pressure."

"I've already got pressure."

"I'll bet if a firecracker went off in here no one would know it. That's Oregon, man. Nothing happens here, even when it does."

"Set one off and you'll never get back on the team," I said.

"I'm not saying I'm going to do it. But I've got an idea for an event you'd never forget."

I thought a moment. "Yeah. They'll either put a plaque on the wall commemorating the event, or they'll put your head on the wall."

Chapter 31

I entered Ivan's room at 11 p.m., moved the open English text that was covering his face to his nightstand, and shut off the lights.

"Burt?"

"You have another roommate?"

"Bad dream."

"Sorry to wake you."

"Anyone see you come in?"

"No. I've got a streak going. How you doing in that Freshman English?" I sat on my bed, leaned back against the wall, and began unlacing my shoes in total darkness.

"How did you do in Freshman English?" Ivan asked.

"A in creativity, C in punctuation. Why?"

"I'm not doing well."

"Aren't you studying?"

"The professor goes too fast. I can't keep up."

"I'll help you if you come to the library after dinner tomorrow."

"Can't. See, I've this girlfriend and she's got this apartment."

"You're having sex all day and night?"

"No. Just when I'm supposed to be in class."

"Ivan, are you saying you stopped going to class?" *Oh shit! He's out—I'm out.* "You better get back in class, Ivan. You have a responsibility to yourself."

Ivan turned away, faced the wall. "I'll work it out."

Worn out because of a lack of sleep, I woke the next morning at 10:00. Ivan was gone. *Maybe all the freshmen on the floor are in class. It's Wednesday. They better be in class.* I quickly entered the white-tiled, communal shower across the hall thinking I would be alone. However, when I turned on the shower, my greatest fear appeared in the person of a guy who was wearing a yellow towel around his torso. I turned away, put my head under the shower and shampooed, hoping he would disappear. But he turned on the shower across from me, and said. "I'm Bob. I haven't seen you around here."

I said nothing, thought: *Jesus! I'm facing away from him. How does he know who's in the shower? By their ass? Go away, Bob!* I let the water flow down my face, didn't know what to say. Tried gibberish. "Buurshma goolan extra folstma."

"Have you just moved in?"

He doesn't quit. I'll just have to kill him. "Exma faca hyberem."

"Who's your roommate?"

"Faca instumaka resofla."

"Are you an exchange student?"

I didn't answer. Minutes passed. I wouldn't turn around. Applied more shampoo. Whatever the guy was thinking, he dried off and left without responding to my language. When the bathroom door swung shut, I ran across the hall, leaving a trail of water spots on the carpet, fearful of silent footsteps all the way.

* * *

That night, I waited for Henry at a central table in the library. Engrossed in my dome stadium project, I thumbed through the annuals of periodicals seeking a lead on "indoor grass," but found nothing. Suddenly, I heard a familiar thudding sound in the distance that echoed in the great hall. My eyes jogged to the sound and my heart sank. There was Henry, all six-three of him, dressed in Padovan's dark green game uniform, number 25, dribbling with all he had down the main aisle. In no time, he sped past me as if he were coming down on a fast break.

"Shit!" I said under my breath. *He said he was going to break the boredom.*

Students around me gasped.

Seconds later, Henry exited the back door, and the library was abuzz with conversation.

"Can you believe that?" said a crew-cut guy sitting across from me.

"What did you see?" I casually asked.

"Come on! A basketball player just dribbled a ball through the library. Where were you?"

"Oh, he did that last year."

"In the library?"

"Yeah. Rumor has it that the guy was cut from the basketball team several years ago and never got over it. Someone said he was committed."

"He should be."

"The guy is a legend around here," I said. "Kinda like the Headless Horseman. Did you get a good look at him?"

The guy gave me a questioning look. "Number 25. He was wearing number 25."

I held back a smile.

The library was quiet again.

*   *   *

I entered the Student Union late the next night and found Henry sitting at a far corner table, incognito with shades and a baseball cap pulled down over his eyes, sipping on his nightly cup of tea. The place was noisy and packed.

I approached him and said over the noisy conversation at the next table, "Where you been, man?"

"Sh-sh-sh," he uttered with a finger across his lips as I took a seat across from him. "I've been letting things cool down."

"Your performance earned great reviews at the library."

Henry took a sip. "It brought more than that. Remember Chuck Mitchelmore?"

"The Christian House guy who's editor of the campus newspaper. Yeah. So?"

"He interviewed me this morning for a story in the *Emerald* about the library dribbler."

My eyebrows shot up. "What did he ask you?"

"He asked if I knew anyone on the team who would do such a thing. I said, "I can't imagine anyone in their right mind doing that.""

"Did he think Padovan did it? You wore his uni." After a beat, I said, "You never handed it in."

Henry's eyes lit up. "I told Mitchelmore that I heard Padovan never went home and is still somewhere in Eugene."

"Did he buy it?"

"I'm not sure."

"Anything else happen about that?"

"Yeah. Belko brought me in to find out what I knew. I told him I didn't know nothing. He said that if I was the crazy one, I was off the team."

"He knows you."

"That's the problem."

Henry glanced over my shoulder. "Now I'm waiting to see what comes out in the *Emerald*."

* * *

The next morning. I got a copy of the *Emerald*. A back-page story began:

PHANTOM PLAYER DRIBBLES
LENGTH OF LIBRARY FLOOR
by Chuck Mitchelmore, Editor

Where do basketball players practice now that the season is over? They go to the library, of course. Two nights ago a man in a Kelly-green Oregon uniform dribbled the length of the library hardwood without scoring a point. The yet-to-be-identified person entered the front door about 8 p.m. Without hesitation he sprinted the floor like he was headed for a basket. Just as quickly, he exited the back door. The dribbler wore number 25, the same number worn by George Padovan, a player who was suspended from the basketball team for breaking curfew on a trip to Cal. Henry Ronquillo, who was also suspended on that trip, had this to say about the library event: "I think that anyone who would do such a thing is crazy. They should lock up the guy before he dribbles down the highway." Basketball coach Steve Belko said, "The matter is under investigation." Barbara Gutkey, head librarian, said, "Never in all my years have I seen such shenanigans."

Chapter 32

The opening meet of the track season at Hayward Stadium against Washington State was the scene of Otis Davis' high jump challenge. A noisy college crowd of about 10,000 filled the sunny side of the stadium, near the finish line for the sprints to cheer the Ducks. Henry and I watched Otis compete from the top row of the crude wooden stands, shoulder-to-shoulder with other students. The high jump was held on the grassy field, directly in front of us. Nothing much was riding on his performance—only Otis's track scholarship for next season, and his graduation.

High jumpers warmed up with the bar at six feet, Otis's highest jump. All the red and white clad Washington State jumpers soared over the bar with ease. Otis cleared the bar by rolling over it with inches to spare.

Watching Otis's every move, I said to Henry, "Maybe this is Otis's time, the day we see him transformed into a big-time high jumper before our very eyes."

He gave me a funny look and said nothing, indicating it would take a miracle.

Ten minutes later, the bar was moved to six-four, the meet starting height. Otis approached the bar for his first attempt. "There he goes," I said. "He's up, and . . . damn, hit the bar with his trail leg."

Flat on his back in the sawdust pit, Otis gazed at the high jump standard, slowly got up, brushed himself off, then stepped out of the pit and walked around the dirt area for a short time with his head down waiting for his next turn. Meanwhile, the other competitors cleared the height with ease.

When it was Otis's turn, he rechecked his steps and practiced his take-off next to the bar by lifting his right knee and throwing his arms up. After pacing off his steps to the bar again, he stood with hands on his knees staring at the bar ten yards away.

All signals go, he took off in a controlled run, planted his left foot short of the bar and went up. But on his way over he hit the bar with his trail leg, and a cheering crowd went silent.

Watching Otis walk head down away from the pit, I said, "Well you just can't be a great high jumper in a month."

"You should have told him that." Henry said, like it was all my fault that he tried high jumping.

"I didn't want to discourage him. And, hey, it's not over yet."

Gazing at the shot put event in progress across the field, I said, "Otis has one more chance. But it's not fair. Everyone else has probably been jumping since they were in high school."

"Maybe earlier than that."

We waited several minutes for Otis to give it another try. If he didn't clear the height this time, he would be eliminated from competition.

Otis went through the run and jump repertoire, then returned to his starting mark as the crowd went silent.

"Okay, Henry, watch him clear the bar. There he goes . . . to the bar . . . up . . . and . . . shit. Hit the bar again."

Displaying no emotion, Otis dusted himself off, put on his green warm-ups and sat on the cold grass near the pit to watch the other jumpers.

Henry said, "Man, this must be tough on him."

"He's got a lot of pride. He'll be back."

We sat in silence as the gun went off for the 100-yard dash. The crowd erupted at the finish. I didn't see who won. A grandstand post that supported the roof was in the way. Having this blind spot got me thinking: *My domed stadium is going to have clear visibility everywhere. But how? I don't know. This project is consuming me just like baseball. Man, are you linear.*

Another thought popped into my head. "We should go to a movie tonight and take Otis."

"I don't have any dough," Henry said, kind of bewildered.

"I'm broke too. But I've got an idea. We won't need any money. And we'll take Otis's mind off the high jump . . . You'll see."

"What's playing?"

"*Bridge on the River Kwai.* I heard William Holden battles the jungle. Something like that."

* * *

Otis said nothing during the drive to the movie house downtown. I glanced at him in the rearview mirror and said, "Well, it's only your trail leg."

We passed two blocks before Otis said, "I want to cut that trail leg right off. Then I could clear six-seven."

"No, you couldn't."

"Yes, I could."

The movie house had an ornate, palatial, Egyptian-style exterior. I cracked the entrance door open. Inside, it was less remarkable. The foyer was simple and small with a candy counter immediately to my right. A red carpet butted up to it. A young lady behind the candy counter sold admissions and concessions. The movie had begun. All the customers were in the theater.

I whispered to Otis, who stood right behind me. "You go in first, buy a ticket, some popcorn and a drink. We'll meet you inside."

Otis said in a low voice, "Okay. But I hope you guys don't get caught."

Otis entered. The young lady behind the counter turned her back to fill the order. I poked Henry and pointed to the floor. We wedged ourselves inside the door and began crawling quietly below the counter, past Otis, the Necco Wafers and the Sugar Daddy Pops to the entrance curtain. For me, the ten-second thrill that came with sneaking in was almost as good as hitting a home run. Although I didn't know it then, I was replacing one exciting thing with another. I needed to be on the edge, to get my heart beating like I did in baseball when I stole a base, made a diving catch, or hit a home run.

When Otis joined us in the smoke-filled theatre, he said in a hushed tone, "You guys have a strange way of taking my mind off high jumping."

I looked around, and could not find three open seats together. "Better head for the balcony."

Otis said sharply. "In Alabama the balcony is the only place I could sit in a white movie house. I'm not going up there."

My head swiveled to him. His comment hit me hard. Memories of Alabama still plagued him. "You'll be sitting up there with white people. This is Oregon, man. Not the same."

Otis finally agreed to sit in the balcony with us and a bunch of white people. We stayed until the movie looped around to where we came in. And I learned a little bit about Otis and the South.

Years later, I learned that I had replaced the thrill of aggressive baseball playing, of loving to play under pressure, with the thrill of sneaking into the show, of taking Henry's test, of being the phantom roommate. Living on the edge was also a need for Henry, Padovan, and Charlie Franklin. But they had to go further out on a limb to get their heart beating. They had to have the big thrill.

Chapter 33

The following Saturday, a miracle happened in the form of a snow-
storm in Moscow, Idaho, although I wasn't aware of its value at
the time. The storm postponed the Oregon–University of Idaho track
meet and made Otis Davis a sprinter. Opposing coaches decided that
instead of rescheduling the meet later in the season, they would run
half the meet at Oregon and half at Idaho the following Wednesday.
Oregon athletes would compare times and distances to determine winners and points for each event. Since there were three more running
lanes available in the 100-yard dash, Bowerman asked Otis to take one
of the lanes. It appeared to me that Bowerman had not given up on Otis
and would experiment with him just like he experimented with track
shoes and running surfaces.

On Wednesday afternoon, the sun's rays were being cooled by a slight
breeze when I watched five Oregon sprinters and Otis, all in Kelly-green
shorts and shirts, line up for the 100-yard dash on the clay track. From
the finish line, stopwatch in hand, my assignment was to clock Otis.
And I was excited to see what he could do.

"Runners to your marks," the starter said, standing outside of the
sprinters.

Otis, on all fours, placed his left foot forward in the starting blocks,
and his right foot back, then reversed their positions. Watching him

closely, I came to realize that he had no idea what the blocks were for.

"Get set," barked the starter. The gun went off.

Unlike Oregon's trained sprinters who bolted out of the blocks at a 45-degree angle when the gun sounded, Otis stood straight up. But he quickly accelerated like a new Corvette, jetting by four other sprinters at the halfway mark.

The sound of spiked shoes grabbing the earth was quickly upon me. And there was Otis, breezing across the finish line ahead of every sprinter except Jack Morris, the star football running back who doubled as a sprinter. After clicking my watch, I looked down for a reading. Astonished, I held the watch above my head and called out, "Coach! Look at this."

The stoic Bowerman strode across the track toward me, his erect posture reminiscent of a military officer, which I had heard he had been during World War II, serving as a sniper in the 10th Mountain Division. After studying the watch, Bowerman said to Otis, who was walking back to the finish line with other sprinters. "Otis, you may be the fastest high jumper in America. Says here you just ran a 9.8."

"Is that a good time?" Otis asked, breathing normally while the other sprinters breathed deeply.

"It is a good time. But we don't know if you were timed with the broken watch." Bowerman fiddled with the watch, then looked at Otis. "I'm going to enter you in the 100 next week against Oregon State and see what you can do. Forget about the high jump."

Otis turned to Jack Morris, Oregon's balding Rose Bowl hero, whose muscles had muscles. "Hey, Jack, did you hear that? It's going to be me and you in the 100 next Saturday."

"No," Morris said. "I'll be first on Saturday."

Otis smiled and said nothing. It was the first time I had seen any sign of satisfaction on his face.

Minutes later, I walked with Otis across a grassy field to the locker room. The sun had begun to set behind the tall pines on the hill behind the track, cooling the temperature significantly. And I noticed that Otis stood taller than he had before his race.

"One thing about starting a new sport," I said, "you have no bad habits to break."

Without altering his stride, Otis laughed. "Yes, and the other thing is I have no habits."

As we made our way to the Mac Court locker rooms, I wondered if Otis had finally found his place in the track world or if running the 100 was going to be just another lark.

Chapter 34

A few days later, I returned to the library and searched through years of the *Periodical Review* for Indoor Grass, the property I needed for my indoor football field. This was the first time I had researched anything except girls' phone numbers. After an hour of tedium, I found an article in *Today's Chemist* that caught my eye. Someone at the Chemstrand Company had developed a carpet fiber that resembled grass in color and texture. The author, Dr. Wright, reported that it could be used for walkways and miniature golf courses. Turning the pages of the thick *Dunn & Bradstreet Directory*, I found a number for Chemstrand.

The next day, at my favorite phone booth in the laundry of my old dorm, I used a coat hanger and a single quarter nine times to call the Chemstrand Company. I asked for Dr. Wright and was connected to the lab.

"Dr. Wright, this is Burt Golden. I'm a student at the University of Oregon and I'm working on a class project. I read your article about carpeted grass in *Today's Chemist* and I have a couple of questions for you."

A deep voice said, "You're the first person in the outside world who has shown any interest in the product. What's your question?"

"This may sound silly, but can the grass carpet you've developed be used for a football field?"

There was a brief silence on the line, before Dr. Wright said, "I never thought about that. With some modification, it could be durable enough, but it would need a mat under it . . . probably rubber . . . Maybe one or two inches thick, glued down to a cement base. Yeah, that could work."

"What if a portable basketball court was on top of it. Would it damage the carpet?"

"Nothing would damage this product in the short term, but I don't know how long it would hold up. But I'm working on a more durable product that will withstand anything."

Dr. Wright went into detail about his grass. I didn't understand a word he said. Towards the end of his dissertation, a woman's voice cut in with, "That will be one dollar for another three minutes."

I hurriedly deposited one quarter four more times, bringing a resounding "ding-ding".

"This must be costing you a lot of money," Dr. Wright said. "It must be important to you."

"Oh, it is. I appreciate your help. And I think I'm really on to something."

"So you want to put my product on a football field?"

"An indoor football field. It's just a concept on paper. But I think it's 'real George.'"

Dr. Wright didn't respond for a beat, and then asked, "Who is George?"

"Sorry. I picked that up on campus. That's a response meaning something is cool, or real good."

A pause. Then "I'd like to see it when you're done."

I thanked him, hung up and smiled. I felt good about the conversation and could hardly wait to tell Henry that I was going to incorporate grass on my field that needed no watering.

*　*　*

On Saturday night, I invited Henry to sleep in Ivan's bed after we snuck into another movie. Ivan had gone home to Portland for the weekend.

After we crawled into the movie house again, we saw *Pal Joey*, starring Frank Sinatra and Kim Novak. A great flick.

About midnight, as we were entering Ivan's room and turning on the lights, Henry said, "You know what? I'm going to call you Pal Jewie."

After clicking the door shut behind me, I said, "Then I'm going to expose you as a Mexican from East L.A., not the Spaniard from Madrid that you've been portraying yourself up here."

Henry giggled loudly.

"Sh-sh-sh. We're not supposed to be here." I pulled out a large cooler from my closet. "I liberated a gallon of frozen strawberries for desert. Also, bowls and spoons."

I sat down on my bed, pried the lid open, and in no time we devoured the contents. When we finished, Henry looked over, his red chin displaying evidence of what went down and how fast. "How did you pull this off?"

"It wasn't easy."

We shut the lights off, got into bed, and I said in a hushed tone, "I'm going to put indoor grass in my dome stadium. It's plastic and won't need watering."

"Man, that's crazy. Sigerseth doesn't like science fiction."

I turned around and dozed off.

In the middle of the night, someone yelling repeatedly awakened me, "Shit on a stick." The voice was somewhere in the hall, coming closer. Seconds later, another guy barked, "Everyone up."

Doors were pounded on, followed by the order, "Everyone up."

In the darkness, I thought: *Maybe a Residential Assistant. Don't move.*

The pounding came closer to our door.

"Damn it," another voice yelled, "Someone put shit on the wall. Everyone up. I'm not going to clean this shit up myself."

The hall became full of anxious voices. Then there was a pounding on our door. "Ivan," the guy yelled. "You have to clean up like everyone else . . . Come out, Ivan!"

More pounding on our door.

"Enough of this shit," Henry said, springing out of bed. He opened the door a crack to a silhouetted figure, grabbed the guy, hauled him in our dark room and slapped him around.

"Ivan . . . Ivan," shouted the guy. "What are you doing, Ivan?"

Then Henry threw the guy out and slammed the door.

No one bothered us again. But I knew Ivan wasn't going to be very popular when he returned.

Chapter 35

With each passing day, the skies became clearer and the temperature warmed. One mid-week day, there wasn't a trace of wind, not a cloud in the sky. After my nine o'clock class, I met Henry on the grassy square across the street from Mac Court. We sat on a park bench soaking up some warm rays while we watched thousands of students stream into the arena. In minutes, the streets and sidewalks were clear, and there wasn't even a pigeon in the square. Only the sound of silence.

Where'd everyone go?" I asked.

"There's some senator speaking. A guy named Kennedy."

"Never heard of him."

"I think he's from Massachusetts."

"Maybe we should hear what he's got to say."

Henry eyed the arena entrance. "He can't be that good."

I looked around at the deserted campus, then leaned back on the bench, felt the sun warm my face and enjoyed the peace and quiet. "You know what, Henry? I'm going to spend more time studying and not hash any more. I'm going to quit my job. It's going to be tight, but I think I can manage through finals. It's taking away study time."

Henry's eyebrows pinched. "Why don't you have your dinners and Sunday brunches at the Philadelphia House? It won't cost you any more than you're paying for dorm food."

"Come on. Do you think they're going to accept Pal Jewie?"

"I won't tell them."

I considered Henry's words. *What's the worst that can happen? I have to buy a sack of potatoes like Charlie? But where would I cook them? No, The Philadelphia House better work.* I remembered playing center field in the late innings when the sun was on its way down. And I smelled the scent of cut grass, another element of the baseball game. I reached down, plucked a few blades of grass and tossed them in air like I used to, in order to prepare for the effect the wind would have on a fly ball in my area. The grass came straight down. Not a hint of a breeze. And I thought: *I'm not half the man I used to be.*

Henry brought me back when he said, "Belko called me into his office this morning. He said I'm not suspended any more. I'm on probation."

"Probation is better than suspension. Did he talk to you about the library incident?"

"Yeah. He asked if I had seen Padovan recently. I told him that I heard he was working at the lumber mill in the next town."

"What did he say to that?"

"Bullshit."

"He knows you're the library dribbler."

Henry studied the pigeon that just landed a few yards away.

"I'm not coming back here," I said. "Are you?"

"I'll talk to Loyola when I get home. They recruited me before I decided to come here."

There was silence again before Henry gave me a snarky look. I had seen that look before. He was thinking about something way out. "If we're not coming back here, we should have a project every day, something to replace the excitement of athletics and the boredom of being a student. Don't you miss it? I mean baseball."

"More than you know, but I'm not dribbling through the library. And I'm not going to jail. I'm getting out of here without a room bill, and I have a pile of transferable credits . . . What do you have in mind?"

"Nothing real bad. Just stuff that would keep this town on its toes."

Stone silence.

"Maybe we should have gone to hear this guy Kennedy." I said.
"Naw."

Chapter 36

The undeclared fastest high jumper in America became a willing experimental sprinter the following Saturday against Oregon State. On a perfect spring day, Henry and I stood against a low, wood rail next to the finish line awaiting Otis's 100-yard race at Hayward Stadium. With no training, other than being told that you "start here and finish over there," he stepped onto the track, unaware that he was about to embark on a very unusual journey. Behind us, a capacity crowd waited silently for the event.

Standing behind the starting blocks, Otis watched his competition. When they touched their toes, he touched his toes. When they shook out their legs, he shook out his legs. When they ran in place, he mirrored them again. Then it was time.

The starter, in a red coat, standing on the infield next to lane one, said loudly, "Runners to your marks." He raised his pistol. The sprinters reacted to his words, "Get set," by rocking forward with their spikes pressing against the starting blocks. They waited a few seconds with tensed muscles for the sound. But none came. Suddenly, one sprinter sprung forward, then another and another. The starter pulled the trigger twice, indicating a false start. Otis was the only sprinter still on the starting blocks. And he stood nonchalantly and waited for the others to come back. The returning sprinters took a long look at him as if to say,

"Who is this guy, anyway?"

Two minutes later, when the gun sounded, the other sprinters got a big jump on Otis who stood straight up before darting off. But by the 50-yard mark, Otis had caught and passed most of them, the crowd roaring in approval. With arms and legs pumping like pistons, Otis managed to finish third.

Henry, his hands on the rail, turned to me. "Wasn't that great?"

"I always knew he was a sprinter."

"Bullshit!"

"But to tell you the truth, I think he should run longer races. He's got great endurance, and he's a slow starter."

Chapter 37

Coach Bowerman usually put on an attention-getting show in class. One of his most memorable performances was when he came through the back door of the room with a quivering, long bamboo pole on his shoulders. With a straight face, he announced, "If you went to the Oregon State meet last Saturday you would have noticed that this pole carried our vaulter above 14 feet. Now clear a path and I'll show you how it's done."

After we moved all the chairs out of the way, clearing a running path, we stood on the periphery of the room as he described the vaulting process. When a student behind him asked a question, Bowerman pivoted, swung the pole around and narrowly missed the student's head. Then, he pointed the pole to the corner of the room and proceeded to plant it as he described a pole vaulter's ascent.

"Watch this," he said, retreating to the doorway and out of the room. Once he was in the hall all I could see was the end of the shaking pole in the doorway. "Now get ready," Bowerman yelled.

The first half of the long pole entered the room, then Bowerman, gripping near the end. He sprinted down the makeshift runway and planted the pole in the far corner of the room, making a solid thud. Bowerman rose a few feet off the ground, the ascending pole hitting the ceiling and removing an acoustical tile, which fell to the floor in pieces. Bowerman landed with a smile on his face, like he got away with something.

I noticed a jagged hole in the corner of adjoining walls where Bowerman had sunk his pole. When class ended, on my way out, I noticed another hole at the other corner of the room. Apparently, Bowerman had struck there as well.

I caught up with Bowerman in the hallway where he marched with the pole on his shoulders and wide-eyed students cleared a path for him. "Coach," I said, walking as fast as I could, "I'm working on a class project for Dr. Sigerseth. "I'm developing a track of the future. What do you think running tracks will be made of in ten years?"

Without breaking stride or looking at me, he said, "They will be made from a mix of rubber and asphalt and it'll be held together with special glue. That's the hard part—developing the glue. I've been working on that myself."

Chapter 38

At mid-week, Coach Bowerman crossed the track to see me as I stood next to the broad jump pit timing the distance runners. "I need someone to cover for our manager this weekend in Seattle," he said. "He had to go home. How would you like to help us out?"

I agreed to take the job because I wanted to see Otis run again, although I had no idea what a manager did. And I heard that the University of Washington was located in a beautiful setting on the shores of Lake Washington. So why not go?

On Friday, in front of Mac Court, I boarded a team bus after loading its baggage compartment with equipment. I climbed aboard, noticed all the athletes had taken seats and spotted Otis, who waved me over. He had saved me a seat. The bus started up, a few girlfriends waved good-bye from the sidewalk, and a busload of crew-cuts drove away.

After many hours of traveling through farm country with green hills that flowed down into the fields, someone tapped me on the shoulder. I turned and recognized a stocky distance runner sitting behind me.

"Aren't you from L.A.?" he asked.

"That's me."

"Ever see Marilyn Monroe?"

"Once. She was driving a convertible next to me, down Sunset Boulevard in Hollywood. Pink T-Bird, dark glasses, and blonde hair flowing with the wind. I waved. She smiled back. I knew who she was. Then I almost rammed the car in front of me."

"I probably would have done the same thing. How lucky you are to live down there."

Lucky? I haven't been lucky for a while.

"I don't know if I could handle L.A. Too many people. Eugene is big enough. Thirty-five thousand. That's a lot more than we have in Grants Pass."

"Tell me about Grants Pass," I said.

"It's a cradle to grave town. You're born there, you die there. The big thing is getting drunk on Saturday night. We just got TV a few years ago. Hey, how many channels do you have in L.A.?"

I thought a second. "Seven. Three networks and four independents. They say in the near future we'll have color TV, but I don't mind the black and white."

The guy shook his head in amazement. "That's a lot." Then he turned to Otis who was gazing out the window. "Hey, Otis, you ready for the Huskies?"

Otis continued to look out the window. "I'm just enjoying the trip to Seattle."

"Don't you get excited about anything?"

Otis shut his eyes and said, "I'll tell you when I do."

*   *   *

Ominous gray clouds and a chilling Lake Washington wind greeted us the next day at the University of Washington after we had spent the night in a downtown hotel. The stadium, which had a capacity of 55,000 was open at both ends and funneled cold wind through it.

Athletes warmed up in parkas and coaches added gloves and ski caps to their attire. Shortly before the first event, the wind stopped and the sun came out, creating a bearable temperature. Then, thousands of fans came out of nowhere and filled about ten rows near the track in time for the first event, the 100-yard dash. I hustled to the finish line and watched Otis record another third place finish. Minutes later, I was speaking to Otis at the edge of the infield grass near the starting line when Bowerman approached and congratulated Otis. Then he said, "I want you to run the 220 today. You'll start in the same place."

I stood there in silence, thinking: *That's a damn good idea. Otis has great endurance.*

But Otis wasn't immediately receptive to the idea, and gave Bowerman a blank stare. Then he looked down the track and asked Bowerman where the finish was.

Bowerman pointed in the distance. "It's down there by the wheelbarrow."

"I don't see it," Otis said. "And if can't see the finish I'm not running. No. That's not for me."

Bowerman's back straightened, as if he wasn't used to being challenged. Then he put an arm around Otis and walked with him to the center of the infield. I did not hear what was said, but Otis returned to the track and twenty minutes later, warmed up for the 220.

When the gun sounded for the event, Otis was slow to explode from the starting blocks again. But with opponents' spikes kicking up dirt in his face, he chased the pack, making up ground with each stride. Midway through the race, Otis shifted into another gear and shot by everyone. The longer he ran, the stronger he looked. At the finish line, Otis was three yards ahead of the closest sprinter, a winner at last.

I saw Otis on the crowned grass infield minutes later. "Nice going," I said, shaking his hand. "This qualifies you for the Northern Division Finals of the Pacific Coast Conference here next week."

He smiled. "Hey, that's okay."

"It gets better. If you finish in the top three, you go to Cal Berkeley for the conference finals."

Otis nodded, and said with all the stress of someone in an upcoming picnic race, "I have some friends in Berkeley. That would be fun."

I remembered his low blood pressure and heart beat scores that he recorded before and after an Oregon basketball game, and I wondered if he ever got excited about anything.

Chapter 39

It was the first of June, 17 days to finals and counting. The closer I came to the end of the quarter and getting the hell out of Oregon to establish a new life, the more consumed I became with the calendar. Henry had finagled the Philadelphia House hierarchy to accept me for lunch and dinner, even though I was not living there. On this day, Henry, sitting beside me at the crowded lunch table, poked me in the arm. I gave him a "what the hell is it this time" look. With a Cheshire cat grin, he opened his green Oregon letterman's jacket, displaying a gun under his belt, next to his hip.

"Whatever you're thinking, it's wrong," I said.

"It's just a track starter pistol. I've been using it at the junior high where I teach."

"Is it loaded?"

"Yes."

Chuck Mitchelmore, sitting at the end of the table with a clear view of Henry, said calmly, "Please pass the bread, Henry, and cite Henry a nickel penalty—he has a pistol. Very bad table manners."

Twelve pairs of eyes shot Henry's way.

Henry slipped out the pistol and pointed it at the ceiling.

Fifteen house members at the table cringed, like they expected a canon to go off.

"It's only a starter pistol," Henry exclaimed. "I use it for track meets."
Quizzical looks came his way.

"Why did you bring it to lunch?" Mitchelmore asked.

"It's a joke. A joke, that's all."

"Please refrain from such jokes in the future."

Henry turned to me and said in a hushed tone, "Let's talk after lunch in my room."

* * *

Henry's room overlooked busy 13th Street. So did his extensive stack of long playing records on his windowsill. We sat across from each other in the bare-bones room, a small box of textbooks on his unmade bed draped with a damp shower towel. I listened to him divulge an idea. It was risky. And like every guy serving fifteen to twenty, Henry had thought it through. Then he added, "I need an accomplice."

Since I was the only other guy in the room, I assumed he was talking about me.

"This place has screwed you," he said, getting my attention. "Now you can leave them something to remember you by."

I questioned if we could get away with it, but there always was a little theater in me. I had some free time. And it would be over in less than a minute. Then I could work on my class project.

* * *

The next day, Henry dropped me off a block from JC Penney in downtown Eugene. He drove my Chevy around the block while I walked to the busy intersection in front of Penney's entrance with my heart in my mouth. Scores of pedestrians crossed at the light as I waited under a warm sun. Two middle-aged women and one young woman stood next to me, apparently waiting for the "go" signal. The young woman stared at me. "Haven't I seen you in the Oregon library?" she asked in a soft tone.

I looked away, not wanting to be connected with the university in any way.

With the passenger window down, Henry pulled up at the corner, almost on top of the curb, pointed his starter's pistol at me, and fired twice.

My upper body slumped inside the opened window.

A woman screamed, "Oh, my God!"

More screams.

Henry pulled the rest of my body inside, and lurched down the street in first gear, as I hung onto the lead edge of the passenger seat. We cornered with tires screeching.

Two blocks later, on a quiet residential street, Henry pulled over and let me into the car. My abdomen in pain from hanging over the window's ledge, I scooted inside and sat down. I reached down and slid the pistol, which was lying on the rubber floor mat, under my seat. Henry floored it, the car jerked forward, and I took a breath. I was over. Then came the siren and flashing blue lights and a black and white pulled us over.

My eyes met Henry's. "Don't say anything until you're accused."

"I'll do the talking," Henry said, rolling down his window.

As the officer approached us, his boots clicking on the pavement, I wondered if I could take my finals in jail.

The officer bent and glared at us though his dark aviator glasses. "Let's see your license," he barked.

Henry looked up at him. "Will you guys make up your mind. Yesterday you guys took my license away. Now you want to see it."

My head rocked back against the headrest. *Goddamn worst thing to say.*

"Both of you out of the car."

"Let me handle this," Henry said in a hushed voice.

"You've done enough."

Outside, behind my trunk, the officer said to Henry, "Why was your license taken?"

"Sorry, I was only kidding."

"Don't play with me, kid, or I'll haul your ass to jail. Now let's see your license."

He doesn't want us for the shooting. We're going to beat this.

The officer studied Henry's license, told us not to move, returned to his car, and got on the radio.

"Don't worry," Henry whispered. "I'm throwing him off the track."

"Just shut up."

The officer returned Henry's license, his ticket pad in hand. "Are you two jerks students at the U of O?"

"Yes, sir," I said, thinking a bomb could still drop.

He scratched something out on the pad, tore it off and handed the ticket to Henry, then like a sentencing judge, said with an edge, "I'm giving you a citation for a broken left brake light. You've got 21 day to take care of it. The information is on the ticket. Now get your asses back to campus. I don't want to see you guys before school ends—do you read me?"

I managed a deep breath.

"Yes, sir," Henry and I said in unison.

We got back in the car, and Henry looked at me with raised eyebrows and wide eyes, which meant "close one."

I said, "I don't have any money to fix the light."

"Don't worry. In 21 days we'll be history."

* * *

As we rolled back to campus in silence, I had two thoughts: *I just did something real stupid and I have to move forward with my project.*

"Drop me off at the Engineering School," I said. "And hide this car somewhere."

Henry quickly replied, "Don't worry. I've got a good spot."

Based on how Henry handled our last episode, I gave him a long questioning look. "Where?"

"The president's parking spot. The paper reported that he's going to an out-of-town conference for a few days."

"You're right. The police would never look there."

"Why are you going to Engineering?" Henry asked as we shot by his house.

"I need to figure out how to hold up the roof in my domed stadium, and I need some help."

Chapter 40

The Engineering School was on the periphery of campus—a brick building with a juniper frontage. I entered a long, dimly lit hallway on the first floor, seeking the dean's office. I did not have an appointment and had no idea who the dean was. All he could do was throw me out.

At the end of the corridor, I knocked on the dean's dark mahogany door and entered a stereotypical bare-bones engineer's hang out. The man behind the desk had a face that appeared to be worn by time. Wearing a white shirt, yellow bow tie and two pens clipped to a shirt pocket, he was leaning forward slightly and reading a thick book, tilted upward on his desk.

The man gave me a questioning eye. "You often barge in on people? This better be important. I'm a busy man. Very busy."

Hoping he would lighten up, I briefly explained my engineering challenge.

"Interesting," he said in a deep voice. "But, son, a lot of students come in here with strange ideas. Last week a young man came by and said he wanted to put a man on the moon. I told him to stay away from Flash Gordon movies." He closed his book. A good sign. Then he said, "I haven't heard of an idea like yours before. You have, as the students say, a 'souped-up' version of a field house." The dean rocked back and clasped his hands behind his head. "Let me ask you this. Why does society need this facility?"

I gingerly slid into the visitor's chair and placed my hands on the edge of his desk. "Dean, imagine a perfect field and a perfect playing temperature in any weather. Fans will always be comfortable and ticket sales will always go up. And all a university needs is one building for football, basketball and track."

He gazed at me for a long moment. "I like that. But I don't know if it's financially practical." He glanced at his watch. "I have a meeting in 34 minutes."

"Well, this is only a class project. I'm not concerned with anyone picking up the concept and running with it." I asked for and received a piece of paper and quickly sketched out a side view of the stadium exterior, leaning on his desk.

The dean studied the drawing. "Challenging," he mumbled. "Are you intending to have grass? You know grass doesn't grow indoors."

"Someone at the Chemstrand Company developed artificial grass."

"Artificial grass. What will they think of next? Let's go on to the structure." He pushed his book to one side. "What are the dimensions of the building?"

"500 by 500 feet."

"Radical. Very radical." The dean pushed off his chair and looked out his window for a long moment. Then he turned back. "You need several bridge spans, wall-to-wall. Then you could lay a roof on top of it."

"Right," I said with excitement, not knowing what the hell he was talking about.

The dean sat down and pulled out a couple of drafting instruments from his bottom drawer. He drew lines going every which way, erased and drew again. Inside of fifteen minutes, he had drawn an inside cross-section of a domed facility with arch supports. I thanked him and walked away from his office with the sketches I had come for. But as he said, engineering stress tests would have to be completed before it could actually be built.

I began to cross the street on my way to the Philadelphia House, several blocks away, to confirm where Henry had parked my car, when a campus police car pulled up and stopped short of the crosswalk I was in. I kept walking but thought it was over. I recalled being pulled over late at night in Boyle Heights for murder. I was returning from a dance, driving my dad's car, with the former student president of my high school and the student body president of a nearby high school. The cop said that the suspect made a getaway in my model, my color car with three people in the vehicle. I explained that he was picking on the wrong people. But that didn't stop him from tearing out the seats and going through everything in my trunk, searching for a rifle. When he didn't find anything, he took us down to Hollenbeck Police Station and had us fingerprinted.

The campus cop waved to me and I waved back.

* * *

On Saturday morning, I read the Oregonian, the state newspaper, in the library. In the local section I found an article that captured my attention. It began:

MID-AFTERNOON SHOOTING IN EUGENE; POLICE CHIEF VOWS TO RESTORE ORDER

The driver of a green 1949 Chevrolet shot a young man at the corner of 5th and Emerald in downtown Eugene. The victim fell into the car and was hauled down the street. Police are working on several leads to find the shooter and determine the condition and whereabouts of the victim. A witness, Barbara Neely, 19, stated that she had seen the shooter dribbling through the University of Oregon library. Eugene police believe there is a connection between the library incident and the shooting. They ask the public that if anyone knows the whereabouts of a George Padovan, former Oregon basketball player, who allegedly dribbled through the library wearing his university uniform.

* * *

A few days later, I moved my car out of the president's space. No tickets. No indication that it should not have been there. From the administration building to the Christian House parking lot it went. And there it stayed for two weeks until the story of the shooting died down in the papers.

Chapter 41

All of a sudden it was mid-June, a week before finals, and I was looking forward to getting the hell out of Oregon. I have to admit, baseball still had a grip on me, but transferring to another university, being ineligible for one year because of the transfer rule, then playing only one season before graduation, was going to be the end of baseball playing. Now I had to grow up and get serious in the classroom. I was closing in on graduation, and very soon I would be seeking a coaching job.

During June, we had southern California weather, sunny and warm. And with it had come the "Rites of Spring" in the form of Saturday night parties. Henry's friend, Bob Doll, told him about a beach party in someone's apartment. But it was invitation only, and we would have to crash. I was all for giving it a go. It would be like my coming-out party. I had had enough of sneaking around campus as the phantom and I needed some joy in my life.

An orange sun was setting when we closed in on the address Bob Doll had given Henry. We rolled down the block until I heard rhythm and blues blaring from what appeared to be an upstairs apartment. Minutes later, I led Henry up a back staircase that made a 90 midway. As I approached the landing on the second floor, I spotted a guy kneeling on top of an exterior storage cabinet, peering through an open window of an outside bathroom. His head was against a sheer curtain and he wasn't visible from the door to the apartment. On tiptoes, I quietly made my way toward him, and pushed his butt with all my might, propelling him through the curtain.

"Oh, shit!" blurted the guy, as he fell into the bathroom headfirst.

"Help!" A girl inside yelled.

Maybe sitting on the toilet below the window.

"That's my girl!" barked a guy inside the screen door to the apartment, a few yards away. The screen door flung open and a big guy, in preppy attire, flew out and ripped open the bathroom door. He was followed by a few other big guys, who rushed by us. While the peeping Tom was being taken care of, Henry and I walked into the party unnoticed. Inside, it was crowded and stuffy, and with each step, I plodded along because of a foot of sand covering the floor. The living room was loaded with couples jiving to Elvis, and the kitchen, a few paces away, was packed with students guzzling beer, oblivious to the rumble outside or the fact that we had just crashed.

Henry and I positioned ourselves next to the ice chests on the kitchen floor. We dug out two bottles of beer, found an opener and drained them. It had been forever since I'd had a beer. And the fact that it was free made it so much better going down. I eyed the coeds dancing in the next room with some big guys, shoulder-to-shoulder. I recognized the football players I had class with but never talked to. By count, there were four football players to every girl, and every girl was dancing with one of them.

A pack of linemen returned from the outside bathroom with their shirttails out, their flattops in place. "Son of a bitch," one guy declared, "a fuckin' peeping Tom."

"Yeah, the Son of a bitch," I said and gulped down another beer.

Soon the party-goers packed the place and the volume of conversation drowned out the music, but nobody seemed to care. I spotted the straight-laced Chuck Mitchelmore in the far corner. He waved Henry and me over. After we shuffled across the room, I greeted him with, "Hey, Chuck, great party."

Mitchelmore quickly jumped all over Henry with, "I want to know about the ex-basketballer, George Padovan. The guy may have shot someone downtown and drove away with the body hanging half-outside his car."

Henry's smile wrinkles turned to worry wrinkles. "You still writing for the *Emerald*? I thought that was over."

"One more issue."

Henry gave me an almost imperceptible glance, as if he was thinking, "the shit has hit the fan," and said to Mitchelmore, "I'll talk to you later about that." Then he pointed across the room. "Hey, Burt, there's Bob Doll. Come on. I want you to meet him."

We weaved across the room in the direction of a guy leaning against the kitchen counter. He was 6′1″, had dark, wavy hair and a twinkle in his eye. An attractive, tall blonde, stuffed into a fitted, green cotton dress had her arms around his neck and a leg around him.

She's slightly overweight, oversexed and over here.

I strained to peel my eyes from her and gave Doll a look. We shook hands.

"Doll is from South San Francisco," Henry yelled to be heard.

"You were in Kines—right?" I said.

Doll frowned. "For a while."

My interpretation: *He dropped the class.*

Trying to be cordial, I said, "Getting ready for finals?"

"A few more drinks and I'll be ready."

"I need three more to get ready and five more to get real over-confident."

Doll, who appeared to have a permanent frown, gestured toward the blonde. "I want you to meet my girl, Cindy."

She turned back to me and squinted like I wasn't in focus. "I'm not wearing my glasses."

Voice like Marilyn Monroe. Lollipops and velvet.

"Cindy is from Eugene," Doll said.

"I'm from Eugene," she repeated.

"She's majoring in psych."

"I'm majoring in psych."

"She finds the U of O boring."

"I find . . ."

"We know," interrupted Doll.

Henry, who worked the crowd as if he was running for mayor, told Doll that he wanted him to meet someone. They crossed the room leaving me with Cindy.

"What's your name again?" Cindy asked.

"I'm Burt," I blared.

She tilted forward, grabbed my shoulder and hung on. "I'm Cindy."

Now face-to-face, wondering how far gone she was, I asked, "How are things going, Cindy?"

"I've got a big problem. How 'bout you?"

Well, I've been shot at, I have to sneak into my room every night, and I'm broke."

"I thought I had a problem."

"How long have you known Bob Doll?"

"We just met."

I gave her a double-take. "He said you're his girl."

"I'm everybody's girl. That's my problem."

Cindy was interesting and entertaining, but I thought it was only a matter of time before I was draped in her vomit. And since my mother told me never to get dirty, I tilted her shoulders back against the wall for safe keeping, and moved on.

Chapter 42

Sitting shoulder-to-shoulder with 20 house members on a hard bench, I patiently waited for lunch to be served with my eyes glued to a front-page photo of Otis. He had just won the Pacific Coast Conference Northern Division 220 race at Washington. A miraculous feat considering it was only the second time he had run the event. That qualified him to run in the conference finals the following week in Berkeley.

I turned to Henry who was to my right, "This is storybook. If Otis places second in the conference meet, he goes to the nationals. Imagine being in that crowd in only a few races."

"Better than the George Padovan story."

Just then, a member who was waving the black instrument called me to the phone at the front door. As the campus phantom, the only people who knew I could be reached here were my parents and Ivan. I picked up the phone.

"Burt?"

A familiar voice. "Ivan, is that you?"

"Yeah. I'm flunking out and going home."

My mind spun. "I'm sorry to hear that. I'm still pulling for you to make it. I'm glad you always keep me up on things. But I'm surprised that this couldn't wait until later, like this evening."

"Because I'm leaving now."

The phone clamped against my ear, I tried to get a grip. *Discovery! Residential bill! Holding up my grades!* "Wait! Ivan, it's not over until it's over. Finals are coming up."

"I'm outta here. And they're going to check my room soon. I thought you'd like to know." Click.

I slammed the phone down and yelled for Henry, who meandered my way.

"Henry, Ivan's going home now! I've got to get out of that room. You're going to help me. Let's go!"

Henry, who loved living on the edge and would create fires to keep his pulse up, calmly let Mitchelmore know we had an emergency and to save us two hamburgers.

Then he got into it, and we ran full tilt to my car, pulled Gs backing up. Then, like it was a four-alarm fire, I tore rubber down 13th Street, my heart pumping like engine pistons. We flew past the men's store that clothed Charlie, past the buffet restaurant where I posed as a player to get a free meal, and two blocks later made a hard right, skidding into the alley below my second story window. I jumped out, clicked open the trunk, sprinted around the building and upstairs. The second floor was dead silent. The freshmen were at lunch but would be back in minutes.

In the room, I jerked open the closet door, ripped my clothes off the pole, ran to the window and tossed them out. Henry caught a couple of items, the rest scattered about. Then pants, more shirts, sweaters, jackets, shoes rained down on the alley floor and the hedge that hugged the building wall. Next, a fifty-pound box of textbooks that ripped apart when it hit the asphalt. Last was my twelve-pound shot put, that smashed into the asphalt, imbedding itself in the blacktop. My mind screamed, "Get out now!" I flung open the door, slamming it against the wall, and flashed across the hallway to the exit stairs.

Back in the alley, evidence of my residency all over the place, Henry and I scooped it up and piled it high into the trunk. With dual pipes crackling, I floored the accelerator, lurched out of the alley and headed back to the Philadelphia House, homeless again.

Chapter 43

Henry and I deliberated in his room for some time, until he said, "Bob Doll doesn't have a roommate, but he's real different."

"What does that mean?"

"The guy's an adrenaline junkie."

"Like you?"

"Worse."

"I just need a place to crash."

Henry placed his long-plays in a large cardboard box. "I have to see Doll anyway. I was in the Jazz Room yesterday when they were taking inventory. When they finished, the supervisor gave me a funny look, like I've got my own Jazz Room. I have to get these records out of here."

I drove Henry and his record collection to Doll's apartment in an unloved two-story a few blocks from the university. Through the screen door, we could see Doll lying on a sofa in a primitive living room reading a newspaper. Henry, cradling about 20 pounds of long-plays, called out to him. Doll didn't move a muscle and said, "Enter and sign in, please."

I creaked open the screen door for Henry and followed him in.

"Okay if I store Burt and these records here for a while?" Doll put down the paper, sat up and gave me a cold look. He gestured to Henry to place the records next to the rifle and map in a near corner. I wondered what the rifle and map were all about, but said nothing, wanting very much to sleep there, no matter what.

After a brief discussion, Doll agreed that if Henry and I helped him pass the Kinesiology final, he would let me stay at his apartment as well as store the records. Doll had two beds, I had the class, Henry had taken Kinesiology. It all made sense to Doll. And with a roof over my head, I wasn't going to argue.

That night I moved in, bringing a change of clothes, a razor and a towel. Several hours later, I was sleeping in a creaky single bed when I was awakened by a slamming door. Maybe a burglar. I sat up, heard footsteps, saw two shadowy figures in the darkness. I recognized Doll's outline, and guessed at the shapely silhouette of the other person.

"Sorry to wake you," Doll said softly.

"That's okay . . . Is that you, Cindy?"

"Hi," she said.

"Don't mind us," Doll said.

I said nothing, but felt awkward, and thought: *What the hell do I say to a guy who saved me from being homeless?* I tried to go back to sleep, but the groaning and interaction from two nude bodies in the next bed kept me awake for a while.

When I awoke the next morning, Doll and Cindy were asleep in the next bed, Clothes were strewn on the floor, as if they had been in a hurry. My eyes jogged to a stream of light coming through a crack in the drapes, falling across my bed. Just then, I heard a door click shut, followed by soft footsteps in another room. I eyed the open bedroom door and waited, wondering if I had only caught the first act of the Bob Doll Show. Then a raspy girl's voice blared, "Hi, Honey. I'm here to clean up."

What a guy! He's got a cleaning service.

Doll muscled into the fastest sit-up I ever saw, jerked the sheet over Cindy's head.

A pretty girl, maybe a coed, wearing a gray sweatshirt and jeans, holding a mop in one hand and a bucket in the other, stepped into the room and froze. She glowered in Doll's direction, and yelled, "You son of a bitch!"

"Sheila, I can explain," Doll pleaded.

You can explain? Really?

"You asshole!" Sheila slammed the bucket and broom to the floor and walked out.

"Who was that?" I asked.

"My girlfriend . . . She'll get over it."

Chapter 44

That afternoon at Hayward Stadium, feeling good about having a bed, while to a point envying Doll's lifestyle, I watched Otis prepare for the conference finals. There were no puddles to be found on the clay track from a passing rain, and the sun peeked through puffy, white clouds and shone on a patch of tall pines on the hill in the distance. Dampness and the scent of wintergreen from "Atomic Bomb" ointment from a few athletes working out filled the air.

Dressed in heavy team sweats, a parka covering his head, Otis jogged in place near the broad jump pit, perspiration rolling off his chin and disappearing.

Wearing a mid-length, wool jacket, stopwatch in hand, I asked if he wanted me to time him.

"No. And I can't stop to talk to you. Bowerman told me to keep moving for two hours. I can run hard or easy, but I'm not supposed to stop. Tomorrow I run repeats until I drop." A smile crossed his face. "Hey, Burt, why don't you get in shape?"

My gut turned over as his comment stirred up memories. "Haven't you heard? Baseball is over. But I'll tell you one thing. If I could run as long and as hard as you I would get in shape. There's no telling how good you're going to get."

Otis gave me a sincere "Thanks, man," and took off down the

backstretch of infield grass. *He is very self-disciplined. Bowerman doesn't have to stand over him and he follows directions to the letter. At twenty-seven years of age, he is just learning how to run the 220 . . . Does he keep getting better, or is this it?*

Chapter 45

At mid-afternoon the next day, Henry and I waited for Otis at a Student Union patio table. The patio was jammed with students taking a study break and catching up on the sun's rays. To accommodate his finals schedule, Otis had worked out in the morning and could hang out with us for a while. While coloring in my dome stadium project with pastel pencils, I looked up for Otis every few seconds, and also joked with Henry about Mitchelmore not digging out enough information about the downtown shooting to warrant an article. I could only handle so many stressors and was relieved that I could remove one from my brain.

Just then, Otis exited the tall glass door of the Union restaurant and started to come our way. Students wishing him well in the conference championships stopped him at several tables. He humbly thanked them for their support and moved on. Otis was now more than a basketball player who was running track. He was this spring's campus hero.

Otis slid into a chair across from me. "Man, there are a lot of students interested in my next race."

Henry said, "Maybe it's your photo on the front page of the *Emerald* that caught their interest."

Otis's eyebrows pinched together. "What photo?"

Henry pulled out a folded newspaper that had been clamped between two textbooks on the table and handed it to Otis who studied his photo. "That's not my best side," he laughed.

"That's a front view," I said. "What's your best side—a back view?"

"No, a shot of me breaking the tape." He glanced at my 8 x 10 stadium sketch in the center of the table. "Hey, Burt, you still working on that dome. You've got to hand it in."

"Just coloring it in. I can hand it in tomorrow."

Henry took a swig of Coke and focused on Otis. "How do you feel about going south to Berkeley?"

I thought Otis was going to comment about winning, but he said, "It should be a great trip. My friends know I'm coming."

He's not excited about the race. But he doesn't get excited about anything.

I asked him, "You ever heard of Willie Whyte?"

"Who's that?"

"He's your competition from Cal who's in the 220. You should introduce yourself to him before the race, because when the gun goes off, you won't see him again."

Otis grinned. "You're digging at me."

"I didn't mean to."

"Yes you did."

Henry said to Otis, "Did you know there's an age limit in the finals of the 220? You can't be older than 26."

"Uh oh. There he goes again," Otis said. Then two beats later, "Burt, are you ready for the Kinesiology final?"

"I'm getting ready by helping someone pass the course who only attended two classes. Henry's also helping."

"You guys aren't that smart."

Chapter 46

Three days to finals, and I was about to use my questionable study habits to help Bob Doll pass his test. That evening, Doll and I sat on his tattered sofa, not a real comfortable place to study but the best choice we had. He cracked open his text, turned a couple of pages, then slammed the book shut. "I need a break. I'll tell you what. Let's break into the Student Union. We can go up there using the underground tunnels. I've been down there and I have a map."

Henry said Doll was an adrenalin junkie. "Not my thing."

"You're no fun."

I ignored that comment, read my notes and the first chapter, concluding that I didn't know what the hell I was doing, but could fake it. Then another thought took over. "Before we get started, I've got to ask you one question. I'm curious. Why did you stop going to class?"

"I don't like school," Doll shot back.

"What do you want to do?"

"I want to own my own nursery like my dad."

"For little kids?"

"No," he laughed. "Plants. I've been working in that nursery all my life. That's what I want to do—be the plant guy." Doll eyed the floor and admitted. "I'm going to school for my dad. He always wanted me to get a degree."

"Okay, let's do this for your dad."

Doll nodded in agreement.

We began on page one and studied deep into the night. I was impressed with Doll's comprehension and retention of information. I was also surprised by how much he knew about the coursework.

About two in the morning, Doll called a timeout and left the room. I thought he was going to the bathroom. I shut my eyes for a moment, and I was out. Then I heard, "Burt!" Doll stood over me with his rifle by his side. My eyes opened wider.

"Look," I said, "if you don't want to study anymore, it's okay with me."

Doll smiled. "I've got this idea." He leaned the rifle against the front door and did a one-eighty. "You know the Buckeye tree?"

Kinesiology, rifle, Buckeye tree. Make some sense out of that. "What the hell are you talking about?"

"At the Rose Bowl game, the governor of Ohio gave the governor of Oregon a Buckeye tree. That tree is planted in front of the law school. I'm taking it home."

"We're cramming for a final . . . You're close to flunking out and you're going after a fuckin' tree?"

With a gleam in his eye, Doll said, "I'll be the only one in South San Francisco with the Buckeye tree. We'll be right back. Won't take a minute. Then we'll study some more."

I was overcome with boredom, and checkmated out. Taking a break was a good idea. Doll wasn't going to hurt anyone. I got into my car with Doll and his rifle, drove a short distance to the law school, parked across the street, but didn't see any tree in front of the school. A bright street lamp lit the sidewalk and the lawn that ran to the brick building. But there was no tree.

"There it is," Doll said excitedly, pointing across the street.

Finally, I made out a three-foot high plant. "That's it? That little plant?"

"That's it. Keep the engine running." He reached back, grabbed the rifle off the back seat, opened the door and crossed the street. Under the street lamp, he aimed high, and squeezed the trigger. The crack of the shot echoed, the street went dark and fragments of glass sprinkled down as Doll ran back to the car. My heart running away with itself, I floored it as soon as Doll's body was in the Chevy. The acceleration threw my shoulders back and streaked down the street. "I'm coming back here tomorrow night to dig it out," Doll said, like he was about to take the beach. "Now let's get some sleep."

"No," I said, swerving around a corner. "Let's make some coffee. If you sleep, you fail."

"You're fuckin' nuts."

"*I'm* nuts?"

Chapter 47

I didn't know if our study marathon was doing either of us any good. But we kept going. When the sun started to rise, Henry showed up with a bag of sweet rolls and coffee that he secured from the house. We devoured the meal around a rickety cocktail table in the living room. Bob Doll finished his portion, closed his eyes and slouched, as if it was all over for him. He didn't respond to Henry's, "Ready to go, Bob?"

After breakfast, Doll's mind appeared to check back in, and Henry took over. I went back to bed and when I returned to the living room at mid-afternoon, they were still studying. And there was a gunnysack and a shovel next to the front door. Upon closer inspection, I saw that the container was filled with wet sawdust and formed a damp ring on the dusty floor.

I ate another roll, this time in bed as I studied for another class. That night, after Henry left, I tried to build on the material I had covered the previous night with Doll. I didn't mention how long he had been study-ing. And the only thing that kept him awake was our talk of returning to the law school and digging out the damn Buckeye tree.

Sometime after midnight, Doll closed his book. "Let's go get the tree."

I said, "Only if you promise to come back here and study after you're finished."

He murmured, "You're relentless," which I took as a yes.

We took Doll's car this time, a dirty two-door '50 Ford. Doll placed the gunnysack and shovel in the trunk. He said it was important that I drive the get-away car, so I did my best with the rusty stick shift.

As we rolled toward the mission, I asked, "What's the sawdust for?"

"The wet sawdust will keep the tree ball alive until I re-plant it in South San Francisco."

Somehow I made it to the law school without falling asleep, although I was close and had to open the window for a cool rush of air on my face. At the law school, an energized Bob Doll sprung from his seat. Armed with his tools he quickly dug up the root ball of the tree and gingerly slid it into the gunnysack, like he had done this sort of thing before. Then he raced back to the car and placed the tree in the trunk.

When we returned to Doll's apartment, he positioned the tree on the porch, staring at his acquisition for a long moment before coming in.

We did not study effectively for the next five hours, but kept plugging along. When the sun came up, Doll was still awake enough to respond to my questions. But I didn't know if his answers were right or wrong.

The third study night was the roughest on us all. Doll's attention was sporadic. He kept nodding off and coming back. Henry took over for a while and I went into a semi-coma. By morning I didn't know if Doll was ready for the test or not, and didn't care. I had had enough of the subject, Doll, and the root ball.

At 8 a.m. Doll and I waited in a large lecture hall waiting for the Kinesiology test to be passed out. Students were seated in every other chair, nothing on their desks except a pencil. Bob Doll was across the aisle from me. His eyes were focused on the front wall. He wasn't blinking.

The professor passed out the exam. I was concentrating on the first page when I heard a loud thud next to me. My tired eyes jogged to the sound. Bob Doll had fallen out of his chair onto the floor. He lay there in a fetal position, fast asleep.

"Bob," I said. "Wake up."

He didn't move.

I waved for the professor who rushed over and checked Doll's pulse. I assumed to see if he had died. But his pulse was normal. A male student came down the row, bent and shook Doll, but to no avail. A stretcher was brought in and Doll was removed from the room.

*　　*　　*

After my two o'clock final in Organization and Administration of P.E., I returned to Doll's apartment. There, I found him fast asleep on the sofa, one leg draped over the backrest. I stood there, motionless. *Nothing I could do for him now. I feel sorry for him, but I kept my side of the bargain. I got to stay here and he was tutored. Now pack up and get the hell out of this rattrap.*

Chapter 48

The next morning it was all systems go. Finals were over, and California was calling. Henry and I quickly loaded my car, which was parked in the back gravel parking lot. I slid my 12 x 24-inch dome project with its detailed views and a scribbled "A" grade on the first page with the comment, "Never happen," in the back seat. Somehow Henry loaded that area to the roof with ten basketballs stamped "Property of Oregon Basketball," which were going to block a rear view of the highway. Henry's records had to go up front. Where he was going to sit, I didn't know.

I reentered the house from the back porch, and shot across the living room to answer the door bell. The last time I would do that. Upon opening the front door, I was face-to-face with a cop who held a rifle dramatically across his chest. At six-two and about one-eighty, he wore a beige uniform and aviator sunglasses on a stern face. "I'm looking for Henry Ronquillo," he barked.

My brain said, *This is about the shooting downtown,* and my heart took off for dear life. I called upstairs to Henry, who ambled down the steps until mid-way when he saw the cop. Then he raised his hands above his head and blared, "I didn't do it."

The cop didn't change his expression and motioned to Henry to join him outside.

I leaned over a sofa, my nose to the living room window, and watched them talk next to the black and white. I thought there was a good chance of Henry being arrested. When the cop pointed his finger in Henry's chest, Henry threw up his hands once more. Then Henry pointed toward town. Minutes later, he returned to the house with an ashen face and motioned for me to join him upstairs.

Climbing the stairs, I thought, *I'm in the clear, but the cop nailed Henry for something.*

Henry did not bother to close his door. "The cop thinks I stole seventy-five records from the Jazz Room. He also said he heard a guy named Burt was my accomplice."

I gave Henry a scorching look. "That's what I get for hanging around with you."

Henry calmly continued, "Don't worry, man. He'll never find you. I told him you were a townie and didn't go to school."

"What did he say then?"

"Bullshit!"

I crossed my arms. "The cop can go to admissions and records and look up my address . . . I gave them my last quarter's address. But now nobody knows where I live. Not even me."

"I'm the one," Henry said, "whose ass is on the line. But the cop said if I returned the records today, he would forget the whole thing. Otherwise, he would go to Belko. Then Belko would cut my scholarship."

"But you're not coming back here."

"I changed my mind. I want to come back."

I walked to the window in deep thought, then turned back. "You can't get in the Jazz Room today to return the records. The Student Union is closed up. School is over."

Henry said, "I'll leave the records by the front door of the Union."

"Someone would take them. You have to leave them at the Jazz Room door."

"How am I going to do that, man? Drop through the roof?" He said sarcastically.

"Bob Doll has a map of the underground tunnels. He's been down there. That's your ticket."

Henry wasted no time taking the stairs, muttering, "Hope he's in town. He's got the records."

We sped down the street in my car, passing scores of students loading up their cars. *Everybody's going home and we were going to jail.*

At Doll's apartment, we found him stuffing clothes into his luggage. He looked up at Henry and said coolly, "A cop came by a couple of hours ago. He asked about some missing long plays. But he didn't notice your collection in the corner or the Buckeye tree on the porch. I'm clearing out. You should too. Take those fuckin' records."

I explained our predicament to Doll, ending with, "You know how to get into the Student Union through the underground tunnels. That's the only way we can return these records."

Doll continued to pack. "That's your problem. I'm outta here."

Henry raised his voice. "We helped you with your final and Burt helped you snatch the Buckeye tree. Now we need your help. You always wanted to break into the Student Union."

Doll stared at Henry for a two count. "That's dead of night stuff. It's broad daylight."

"We'll be in a tunnel, like the dead of night. And no one's in the Student Union. It's locked up."

Doll began to disassemble his rifle. "Yeah. In an odd way, I owe you. But we have to go now. I don't want to get stuck in San Francisco traffic on the way home."

Henry glanced my way with a worried look, like no one would bet on this long shot.

Doll grabbed a flashlight and map from the kitchen counter and briefly studied the tunnel's pathways. Then Henry loaded the box of records in Doll's trunk. Two blocks later, we pulled up to a white church that was in need of paint.

A small cement block building occupied the far end of the church parking lot, maybe five feet wide, five feet long, six feet high. A metal grate served as a door. As we marched toward it, I noticed a deteriorated shackle of a broken lock hanging from a heavy chain.

Doll said, "I shot the lock off to get into the tunnels last month." Doll twisted and removed the lock and opened the grate. We edged down narrow cement stairs to what could have been a tunnel. The only light came from the glow of Doll's flashlight.

Darkness,

Stone silence,

Musty air.

Something netted my face. I quickly brushed off a large cobweb and the something that was trickling down my cheek.

Doll lit up the darkness, disclosing a narrow wood bridge in front of us, as well as a myriad of pipes on the ceiling that seemed to run forever. The ceiling was about seven feet high.

"Jeez, it's warm, Henry," I said.

"Steam tunnel," Doll said, as the point man. "This place heats up the whole university. Watch out for the high-voltage lines."

"Nobody dies," I said.

Doll led us single file down a one-laner. Henry trailed, lugging the box. After about a hundred claustrophobic yards, we came to a T in the walkway. Doll sprayed light on his map. "Okay, turn left."

Following his instructions, I soon heard hissing and clicking noises somewhere in the distant darkness, and wondered what the hell it was. The farther we walked down this tunnel, the louder the noises and the hotter it became.

I walked past a "FUCK FDR" sign splashed in white paint. A large overhead pipe was in front of us, about six-feet up. I walked under it without ducking. Doll and Henry had to crouch down. Several minutes later, we came to another T in the walkway.

Louder noises,

Hotter temperature,

Damper air.

"Hold it," Doll ordered, stopping to read his map again. "It appears . . ."

"It fuckin' appears!" I interrupted, my body now a sweat machine.

"Relax, and keep going."

The hissing and clicking sound became louder with each step.

192

"What's that noise, Bob?" I asked.

"Just steam shooting out of a busted valve that could melt you. This is as far as I came last time. Isn't this a kick in the head?" His flashlight brightened a stream of steam shooting across our path to the wall, about chest high.

Everything inside me screamed, "Turn back."

That's when Henry declared, "I'm not going through that shit."

"This is insane," I said. "This isn't about the records any more. It's about survival."

"We can get through this," Doll said, his voice no more comforting than the boiling steam in front of us. "Listen to the sounds."

If I get through this, I swear, I'll lead a quiet life.

In a few seconds, the hissing and line of hot steam stopped. Then came the clicking.

Doll said, "There's a sequence to this thing."

"If you're wrong," I said, "I'll have another hole in me."

Steam shot across the path again.

"There's about twenty seconds of clicking," Doll said, "followed by a burst of steam of about nine seconds. Get your asses through when the clicking starts up again."

"I want a recount," Henry said.

Doll counted out loud. "Yeah, twenty seconds of life followed by nine seconds of death."

When the clicking started up, Doll shot across the kill zone, turned back and shone light on the walkway for us to cross.

Suddenly, my legs felt as heavy as cement. But I forced myself forward, followed by Henry. In seconds, we were beyond death's door.

"Burt, help me with this box," Henry said. He handed me the box in the darkness, the flashlight pointing away from us. I hoisted the box of plastic on my shoulder, and I hustled to keep up.

We passed a storage room flush against a concrete wall, when Doll stopped and said, "This is the thrill of the thing . . . I'm not sure where we are."

I took a deep breath. "I knew it. You have a death wish!"

Henry proceeded to review with Doll each of the turns we had made. His memory was amazing. Doll walked his fingers across his map. "Here we are. We've arrived. Right under the Student Union." He pointed at a dark corner. "And here's the door."

What if it's locked?

Doll tried it. It didn't budge.

I knew it.

Then Doll thrust a shoulder at the door, loosening it up. Then he creaked it open with all his might. We proceeded to climb a narrow wood staircase, flicking off the cobwebs all the way. At the top of the stairs was another door that Doll opened. He peeked out. "We're next to a loading dock." We all entered the far end of the Student Union and listened to the silence.

Doll's map didn't include a top-view diagram of this building, and it took a few minutes for us to get our bearings. Our tennies squeaking with each step, we found our way inside the bookstore. Doll went to one of the counters. "Hey! Do you guys want some sweatshirts?"

I said, "We've already got breaking and entering. I don't want any more charges if we get caught. Let's go to the Jazz Room."

Doll snatched an emerald green Oregon sweatshirt and put it on. "I didn't come all this way for nothing."

We hustled down the hall to the Jazz Room door, which Henry tried with no success. "Damn," he moaned.

The record box still on my shoulder, I set it down next to the door. "Let's get outta here."

"Back to the tunnels," Doll said.

"No. Each of us will exit a different door at the same time. We'll count to twenty, get to a door and leave at the same time. I saw this in a movie. If the alarm goes off, they can only catch one of us."

"There are no alarms," Doll said.

"How do you know?"

"It's a long story."

We started the count. I went out the restaurant door onto the patio at "20," and then caught up with Doll and Henry around the block. But

I was concerned with Doll's conspicuousness. *Who walks through a deserted campus in broad daylight, holding a flashlight in one hand and a map in the other?*

*   *   *

Back at Doll's apartment without incident, Henry and I helped him load his car and set sail for South San Francisco. As Mr. Excitement sped away, I felt a release of tension and turned to Henry. "I'm glad this is over. I'm going to go home, transfer to a local college, graduate and get a secure job."

Henry reacted with, "I don't think so."

Chapter 49

Two years later, I was finishing my degree at Cal State Los Angeles as a transfer student.

My twelve-year romance with baseball had ended like two lovers who had repeated separations and reconciliations before breaking up. Tearing an ankle while running after a fly ball for CSLA ended my senior season and helped me come to that decision, as well as hobbling around campus for eight weeks in a leg cast, thinking about my future.

During these long moments of inaction, I came to the conclusion that I had another love—coaching. And I thought I would be a more successful coach than a player. Strictly a hunch bet. But during my eighth and last week of living with a leg cast, I made my usual entrance to my English Lit class, moving my crutches a short distance forward before swinging my body frontward, I plopped into a chair in a far row, without any idea why I was there, or what the future had in store for me.

I looked up for the professor and spotted a guy coming down my row holding a notebook in one hand and a *Sports Illustrated* magazine in the other. He took the chair in front of me. I tapped him on the shoulder. "Mind if I borrow your magazine for the hour? I'm failing this class and should have dropped it. I won't bother you."

It was a strange situation. Although I had never flunked a class, I was ill-prepared to take this upper division course that the newly-minted professor had made into a graduate class. But, as usual, I didn't quit. A positive and a negative habit that I had all my life.

The guy handed back the magazine without a word. I thanked him and turned its pages looking for something of interest. Minutes later, the instructor entered, and with a lisp that would drive anyone crazy, she began to conduct our course. And I just sat there thinking: *Graduate next semester while student teaching and working on your masters. Then who is going to hire you? You only know baseball and you need to know two sports well to get a coaching job. You've got a problem.*

Half-listening to the instructor repeating a line from Shakespeare's *Othello*, "Put out the light and then put out the light," I thought, *I really don't give a damn if Othello knocks off Desdemona.* Then I came across a three-page story about Bob Cousy's Graylag Basketball Camp in the White Mountains of New Hampshire. Cousy had just been voted the best player in the first 50 years of basketball, and he was the floor leader of the NBA champion Boston Celtics. A light bulb went on in my head. The answer to my coaching future was to work at that camp, be educated by Cousy, and become a proficient basketball coach.

I took out a piece of three-hole paper and wrote a letter to Cousy in care of the Boston Celtics at Boston Garden declaring my interest in working at his camp and had the audacity to say, "I will help you if you help me." That afternoon, I typed out the letter and mailed it. Two weeks later, I received a letter back from Cousy's partner, Fred Geib, with employment instructions.

I was hired.

* * *

But you see, old dreams don't die easily—they have to be put to rest. A couple of weeks later, after recovering from my injury, I played in what I thought would be my last baseball game, a semi-pro contest against a former minor-league pitcher. And I hit the hell out of the ball. After the game, I came off the field knowing that I could still do it, a good feeling to end it all.

As I gathered my gear in the dugout, Dodger scout Kenny Myers, who had shown interest in me during the winter, approached me. A stocky man with a serious look and an unlit cigar in the corner of his mouth, he said, "Burt, I'd like you to play for my team, the Dodger Rookies. I want to work with you and send you out." Words I had wanted to hear all my life. Baseball had been my life since I was in the fourth grade, and I was a Dodger fan. He was saying I could be a Dodger, one of 700 minor leaguers in the organization who could work their way up to the show. Myers was one of the great minds in baseball, one of the game's great fundamentalists.

Could I?

Kenny wanted to coach me, spend his valuable time with me, and up my game. I stood in the makeshift dugout behind a chain-link partition facing someone who could change my life, my mind spinning. I knew the routine. Myers had developed my friends and former teammates Ernie Rodriguez, Conrad Munatones, and Carl Brio before signing them to a Dodger contract. The Dodger Rookies were a semi-pro team composed of minor league Dodgers during winter ball, and young prospects that were being developed during the summer. I just couldn't make up my mind. Go 3,000 miles to be a coached by someone I didn't know, in an environment where I had never been, surrounded by players and coaches proficient in the game, or be a Dodger.

As the seconds ticked away, my decision was tested. I knew deep down inside I could be a better coach than a baseball player, and which career I would enjoy more. I took a deep breath, looked him square in the eyes and said, "Thank you, Kenny, but this was my last game. I'm going to be a coach."

I don't think anyone had ever turned him down before.

*   *   *

Three weeks later, I began my adventure to Cousy Camp, taking my first plane ride to a place I had never been, to work with people I did not know, to eventually get a job I knew hardly anything about. It was the beginning of a pattern I would have for the rest of my life.

After landing in New York and traveling by train to Concord, New Hampshire, I was picked up by one of the camp counselors, and we headed for Camp Graylag, high in the White Mountains, in the noisiest Volkswagen van ever produced. All we had to do was take a route where there were no street signs or camp signs, an eventful ride for a city guy. As I recalled, we turned right off the highway at a Howard Johnson's Restaurant, proceeding past two miles of farms before turning right at a yellow house, then continuing for several miles past more small farms, then turning left at a red barn and continuing on a bumpy, one-lane dirt road that cut through a dark forest and seemed like it would never end. Finally we bounced into the 140-acre campground, which included many rustic buildings and six floodlit basketball courts, nestled next to a 100-acre lake and surrounded by a forest of tall hemlock trees. I stepped out of the Volkswagen with two exceptionally large pieces of luggage, and inhaled fresh, pine-scented mountain air, heard birds chirping and basketballs slapping against a nearby asphalt court. Very different coming from a city known for clutter, traffic jams, smog, and few outdoor courts.

After leaving my bags in my eight-bunk cabin close to the road, I attended a counselors' meeting in a large dining hall with a number of successful eastern high school coaches and players from Duquesne, Colgate, Harvard, Providence, and Brown. I was in heavy company. I had only coached elementary school teams and was a substandard high school basketball player. But I wasn't taken aback when the attendees were standoffish. I knew I was a basketball nobody. I thought, somehow, I would change their attitude during the two four-week sessions and the one-week camp after Labor Day for high school seniors. During the meeting, I learned that my job would be waterskiing instructor and that I would have no coaching responsibility. In other words, I was low man on the totem pole with a nonexistent basketball trust level. And although I didn't show it, I was pissed. I didn't come 3,000 miles to water ski. And I sat there thinking: *How in the world am I going to become more proficient at the game of basketball if I am on the outside looking in?* But

I said to myself: *Somehow, someway, I'm going to change that.* I decided that I would get Bob Cousy's recommendation for a basketball coaching job. It was a matter of swimming against the current once more.

As far as my waterskiing job was concerned, I had never water-skied in my life and thought that would be a disaster.

I sat in the lodge with an empty feeling, learning that the campers' main focus would be playing or receiving coaching, and in their spare time waterskiing, horseback riding, playing board games, or watching TV in the recreation building. There would be an hour rest period in the cabins after lunch to write letters home or nap.

Each counselor was housed with eight to ten campers at one of the ten cabins. That job turned out to be getting them to make their beds and getting them off the courts for lights-out time at 9 p.m.

Surprisingly, I applied the waterskiing process that one of the directors taught me and managed to get all the campers up on skis all summer.

Initially, I talked basketball to Bob Cousy when we were both free. Sometimes we would talk extensively about shooting, development of new offensive moves, leading the fast break. Then I would retreat to my cabin where I would make notes of our discussions for future use. During that summer, I also took notes from Bill Sharman's shooting lecture when he visited, and Coach Red Auerbach's lecture on winning. Then Cousy's Holy Cross coach, Buster Sherry, visited and was kind enough to give me his offense and spell out the high level of aggressiveness he required from his players.

In between sessions I hitched rides with other counselors and traveled to Vermont, Boston, and vacation areas of Hampton Beach, New Hampshire, and Cape Cod. It turned out to be the best summer I had as a young man.

At camp, I was on 24/7, whether I was in the cabin, on the water, on the court playing 5-on-5 on Cousy's team or talking ball to Cousy. One afternoon at camp I had some time off and chose to cross the campground and enter the knotty pine interior of the recreation building for some TV time. There, I turned on the black and white TV. Up came a stadium scene. I sat back in the first of five rows in a hard chair, and heard, "We are back at Stanford Stadium in Stanford California, for the 1960 Olympic Trials. And now the finals of the 400-meter run." I was all set to enjoy the event for an hour, until I was on again. The camera zoomed in on the runners stretching and running in place behind the starting blocks. When lane assignments were announced, my ears perked up when I heard, "And in lane number 5, Otis Davis, of the Emerald Athletic Club in Eugene, Oregon. Davis is the winner of the National AAU 400 meters."

My mouth dropped, my eyes opened wide. I had read the previous spring that Otis was running the 440 for Oregon and recording 47s, an excellent college time. But I had no idea he had won the national AAU title. "And there they go," the announcer said. "One lap. The first three places go to Rome."

I leaned forward on my chair, hoping that Otis would make the Olympic team. The race was over so damn fast, with Otis barely edging out someone for third place. I was overjoyed. Otis had made the Olympic team, and he was going to Rome. You don't know this, but here was a great athlete who was dropped from his basketball scholarship only to become an Olympic athlete. A great story, I thought.

Later, I learned from *Sports Illustrated* that Otis was a dark horse because he didn't know how to pace himself. But I was still happy that he was making the trip and looked forward to watching his race on TV in October.

*   *   *

Two other good things happened to me at Camp Graylag. One, Cousy named me coach of the camp team that participated in an All New England Tournament held at the camp, quite a compliment, since I was chosen over a number of successful high school coaches at camp who wanted that job.

But I had to live through being second-guessed by Cousy in the first game, as he made coaching suggestions over my shoulder. Irritated during the game, I knew that if I continued to let him be my crutch, he would never know if could really coach. So after the game, I marched up to him and blurted, "You appointed me coach, now let me coach. Win or lose, it's my responsibility. I can do this. Now let me alone."

Cousy said, "I didn't know you were so sensitive."

"Just let me coach," I said, "and I'll do a good job."

And I did a good job, winning the tournament, and beating a 7-footer in the finals with only one player over six feet.

I got my recommendation from Cousy.

Chapter 50

"Coach!"

My manager's voice jarred me back to the present. Speed walking toward me, he said, "We're boarding the bus and heading back to the hotel."

"I'm going to walk back to the hotel."

The manager came closer, stopping at the display of noted Oregon athletic champions. He glanced at Otis's photo. "Did you know him?"

"Oh, yeah."

"I know you played baseball here, not basketball. So how did you become a basketball coach?"

"I'll tell you at team dinner. Right now. I need to walk."

Walking was a tension reducer, something that was part of my routine before and after games. Outside of the arena, the air was cold and crisp. Perfect for a long walk.

I walked past the ticket booth area where Otis had yelled to me, "Coach Belko wants to see me about something." Past the entrance to the P.E. building where Charlie Franklin showed Henry and me his dismissal letter. Past the park where Henry and I sat, trying to put our lives together and wondering why all the students were rushing into Mac Court to hear a guy named Senator Kennedy from Massachusetts. And past the underground tunnel entrance that would lead me to a new life.

*Otis Davis setting a world record when he anchored
the 1600 meter relay team at the 1960 Rome Olympics, one day
after he set a world record in the 400 meters.*

Epilogue

OTIS DAVIS, who never gave up, went on to set a world 400-meter record at the 1960 Olympic games. The next day he anchored the 1600-meter relay team to a world record.

HENRY RONQUILLO went on to earn a PhD and received national acclaim while serving 20 years as principal of Roosevelt High School, our old Los Angeles high school.

CHARLIE FRANKLIN became a cop at San Francisco International Airport. He died at an early age.

BILL BOWERMAN, who never gave up trying to create a new type of running track and a new type of running shoe, co-founded Nike and created the modern running track.

CHUCK MITCHELMORE became editor of the *International Herald Tribune* in Paris, France.

GEORGE PADOVAN returned to San Pedro, where he became a long-shoreman. He coached kids' basketball teams for decades.

BOB DOLL returned to South San Francisco and went into the nursery business. It is said that the large tree outside the entrance to his nursery is the Buckeye tree.

BOB COUSY continued leading the Celtics to several more NBA titles before coaching Boston College and the NBA Kansas City team. He was an early inductee into the Basketball Hall of Fame.

KENNY MYERS continued to develop players for the Dodgers. His greatest accomplishment was turning Willie Davis, an average high school baseball player with big-time sprinting ability, into a major league star. Kenny died at an early age.

ERNIE RODRIGUEZ graduated from UCLA and played AAA baseball. He then became a major league scout and managed minor league teams and coached baseball at his old high school. He is in the UCLA Baseball Hall of Fame.

JOAN ORSHOFF became Joan Marks and served as an elementary school principal for many years.

JOE KAPP became the only player to quarterback a team in the Rose Bowl, Canada's Gray Cup, and the NFL championship. He went on to coach football at Cal.

USC had fully desegregated their football team by 1970. The basketball team soon followed.

*   *   *

AS FOR ME, I learned my trade, a stumbling 5-foot-8 ex-baseball player with a passion for strategy. With time, study and a ton of effort, I grew from assistant high school basketball coach to head coach, turning losing programs into winners, developing a high school All-American and winning numerous championships before taking the Boise State job. Along the way, I was fortunate to meet a good-looking, highly intelligent young lady who had a great personality. Maxine had the same adventurous spirit that I had and was very supportive. My two kids, Dane and Jay, grew up to be writers themselves, but not before hearing, over and over again, the stories of my younger years at the dinner table.

I coached basketball for 20 years, a life filled with shooting techniques, defensive strategies, and our share of antics as I worked to grow young men into their greatest selves. In time, however, I grew tired of the travels. I went into business, helping leaders to transition into careers that they loved. It wasn't so different from coaching.

It would be years before I would pick up a pen to write about those times back in Eugene when I sought out a dream that was never to be, and how it somehow guided me to a greater life.

NOT THE END

At Graylag Camp. I was on the far left. Buster Sherry, who also mentored me at camp, is wearing the baseball cap. Bob Duffy, a camp friend who went on to play in the NBA, is wearing a dress shirt.

Learning from Bob Cousy at camp.

My East Los Angeles College baseball team was conference champion.
I am the left-hander sitting in the middle of the first row.

*Boise State timeout: me at center stage, coaching our team at a timeout
against Washington State, a team we went on to defeat.*

*Boise State's Danny Jones going up for a jumper against
Las Vegas in the NCAA Tournament at Oregon's Mac Court.*